I0820501

EXTRAORDINARY ISLANDS

An Atlas of Unlikely Places

IVY PRESS

Quarto

First published in 2025 by Ivy Press,
an imprint of The Quarto Group.
One Triptych Place, London, SE1 9SH,
United Kingdom
T (0)20 7700 9000
www.Quarto.com

EEA Representation, WTS Tax d.o.o., Žanova ulica 3,
4000 Kranj, Slovenia www.wts-tax.si

A catalogue record for this book is available from the British Library.

ISBN 978-1-83600-577-3
Ebook ISBN 978-1-83600-578-0
10 9 8 7 6 5 4 3 2 1

Illustrations by Bob Venables
Design by Mat Wiggins
Publisher: Richard Green
Editorial Director: Jennifer Barr
Editor: Katerina Menhennet
Art Director: Patrick Carpenter
Production Controller: Alex Merrett

Printed in Pontian, Johor, Malaysia PC062025

EXTRAORDINARY ISLANDS

An Atlas of Unlikely Places

Alastair Bonnett

Contents

Introduction ... 6

STRANGE ISLANDS

TANA QIRQOS: *Sacred Island of the Ark* ... 10

TANNA: *'Cargo Cult' Island* ... 16

SANTA CRUZ DEL ISLOTE: *The Big Horizons of a Crowded Island* ... 22

CHARS OF ASSAM: *Unsettled Islands* ... 28

KIHNU: *Island of Women* ... 34

SAMSON: *An Island Back in Time* ... 40

OCEAN FLOWER: *A Modern Fairy Tale* ... 46

MALDIVES FLOATING CITY: *Islands of the Future?* ... 52

SCARY ISLANDS

RUNIT: *Monster Island* ... 60

POVEGLIA: *The Horror and the Lies* ... 66

ANAK KRAKATAU: *Child of Krakatau* ... 72

FIRE ISLAND: *Russia's Prison Island* ... 78

BRP SIERRA MADRE: *A Frontline Island* ... 84

BARQUE CANADA REEF: *Vietnam's New Military Islands* 90

REMOTE ISLANDS

FORT JEFFERSON: *America's Distant Fortress* 98
INACCESSIBLE ISLAND: *The Farthest Shore* 104
NORTH SENTINEL ISLAND: *Modern Survivalists?* 110
YESTERDAY AND TOMORROW: *A Cold War Across Time* 116
AASTA HANSTEEN: *Mega Rigs at the Edge of the High Seas* 122
SAN NICOLAS ISLAND: *A Story of Survival and Loss* 128
SOCOTRA: *Dragon Blood Trees and Fighter Jets* 134

NATURALLY ODD ISLANDS

MAYDA INSULA AND THE MAGIC ISLANDS OF TITAN: *Extraterrestrial Shores* 142
A23a: *A Travelling Island* 148
KĪPUKAS: *Islands Surrounded by Lava* 154
FERDINANDEA: *A Fleeting Island* 160
TUPPIAP QEQERTAA: *Discovering a New Island* 166
FLOATING ISLAND: *Natural Wonder* 172
PUMICE RAFTS: *The Ocean's Transport Islands* 178
ÎLE RENÉ-LEVASSEUR: *The Eye of Quebec* 184

Bibliography 190
Index 192

Introduction

WE'RE GOING TO twenty-nine very special islands: every one has an extraordinary story to tell. We start our journey on a tiny Ethiopian island called Tana Qirqos, which is said to have been the resting place for the Ark of the Covenant and, centuries later, was believed to have been visited by Mary and Jesus. It is largely unknown to the outside world, but has witnessed generations of prayer and pilgrimage, and its stones are soaked with strange, sad and inspiring tales.

All these islands defy expectations. Take Tanna, a Pacific island famed for its 'cargo cults' and 'worship' of Prince Philip. Neither label is accurate. Or Santa Cruz del Islote, which has been called 'the most crowded island in the world' and depicted in internet clips as hell on Earth. A different picture emerges if you take the time to listen to its people – in this case the clichés are wrong. Santa Cruz del Islote is super-crowded but, like so many small islands, it's a place of big blue horizons and is intimately connected to a far-flung archipelago.

From strange and surprising islands, we move to scary ones. But they, too, ask questions and, once again, clichés are debunked. Take Poveglia: today it's one of Venice's uninhabited islands and billed on schlocky TV and YouTube exposés as 'the scariest' and 'most haunted' place on Earth. When you look deeper, and listen to locals, it turns out the real story is kookier. Yes, it was once home to an asylum but no, the soil is not made up of the bones of the unhappy dead. Other 'scary islands' are more genuinely frightening but they also carry untold stories. The Pacific island of Runit is a truly fearful place: it has been bombed more often and more thoroughly than any other place on Earth and is dominated by a monstrous leaking 'tomb' of radioactive waste. Yet today the indigenous people who lived on the once-idyllic loop of coral islands that cradles Runit are reclaiming and resettling their mutilated homeland. Another island not for the faint-hearted is Russia's prison for killers, 'Fire Island'. Yet, even on this marooned, watery dungeon, there are tales to tell; narratives of love and salvation.

It's invariably humans and how they treat each other that make an island terrifying. This is just as true for volcanoes as it is for prisons. Krakatau is the most famous volcanic eruption in history. What is less known, though far more important to know, is that the volcano that now sits in its place, Anak Krakatau, is likely to be more deadly. This isn't because it's bigger and badder: it's because millions of people now live in the potential impact zone. What is terrifying is not Anak Krakatau, but the human conceit that it can be ignored.

We turn next to remote islands. Not just a bit remote, but in most cases way beyond the compass. There are thousands to choose from, if by 'remote' we mean a long way from a lot of people. The islands we're heading to are distant in more ways than one. Take Yesterday and Tomorrow. In the freezing waters of the Bering Strait, which separates Alaska and Russia, we find two tiny neighbours: one island called Yesterday and another Tomorrow; one American and the other Russian. These twins are cut asunder by nationality and the International Date Line but they tell the same tale, of how indigenous people in the Arctic tried to navigate Cold War geopolitics, and how ongoing political conflict continues to slice families in two.

For island lovers North Sentinel is a more familiar territory. The last 'uncontacted' island tribe on Earth lives here, and they have been the subject of many articles and a few films. I return to this story because it has become clear that far from being 'uncontacted', this tribe, along with the wider community of indigenous Andamanese, know all too well the meaning of contact. They know it means, at best, cultural obliteration; more likely, it means death. The Sentinelese are not Stone Age remnants, living in ignorance of the wonders of the modern world. They are survivalists, hanging on by a thinning thread.

Nature creates the most extraordinary islands of all. Having deep-dived into strange, scary and remote islands we conclude our adventure with the naturally odd. We start off-Earth, on the newly discovered islands of Titan, one of Saturn's moons. The discovery of lakes, seas and islands on this distant planet radically recalibrates the study of geography. Titan is a very strange cousin of Earth: deeply peculiar but still family. Each of the natural islands we will be learning about has this uncanny familiarity. There are natural islands surrounded by lava and ones that float, others that come and go, as well as islands that have only just been discovered. With the retreat of ice at the poles, islands that have been hidden for tens of thousands of years are being revealed. The newly exposed island we will travel to was found in 1993, and has been named Tuppiap Qeqertaa. Though at time of writing it's still not yet made it to Google Earth, you can find it off the east coast of northern Greenland. It's one of many new islands in these high latitudes, and one of very few that has been visited by humans and been given a name.

There is delight and adventure in store. We're headed to some of the farthest, wildest places on the planet: the strange, scary, remote and the naturally odd. It's a roller-coaster ride, so buckle up; there are plenty of surprises. Some make for fascinating trivia but others are more weighty. We're setting sail to small, far-away, disregarded places but each, in its own way, has a tale to tell about how and why the Earth is changing.

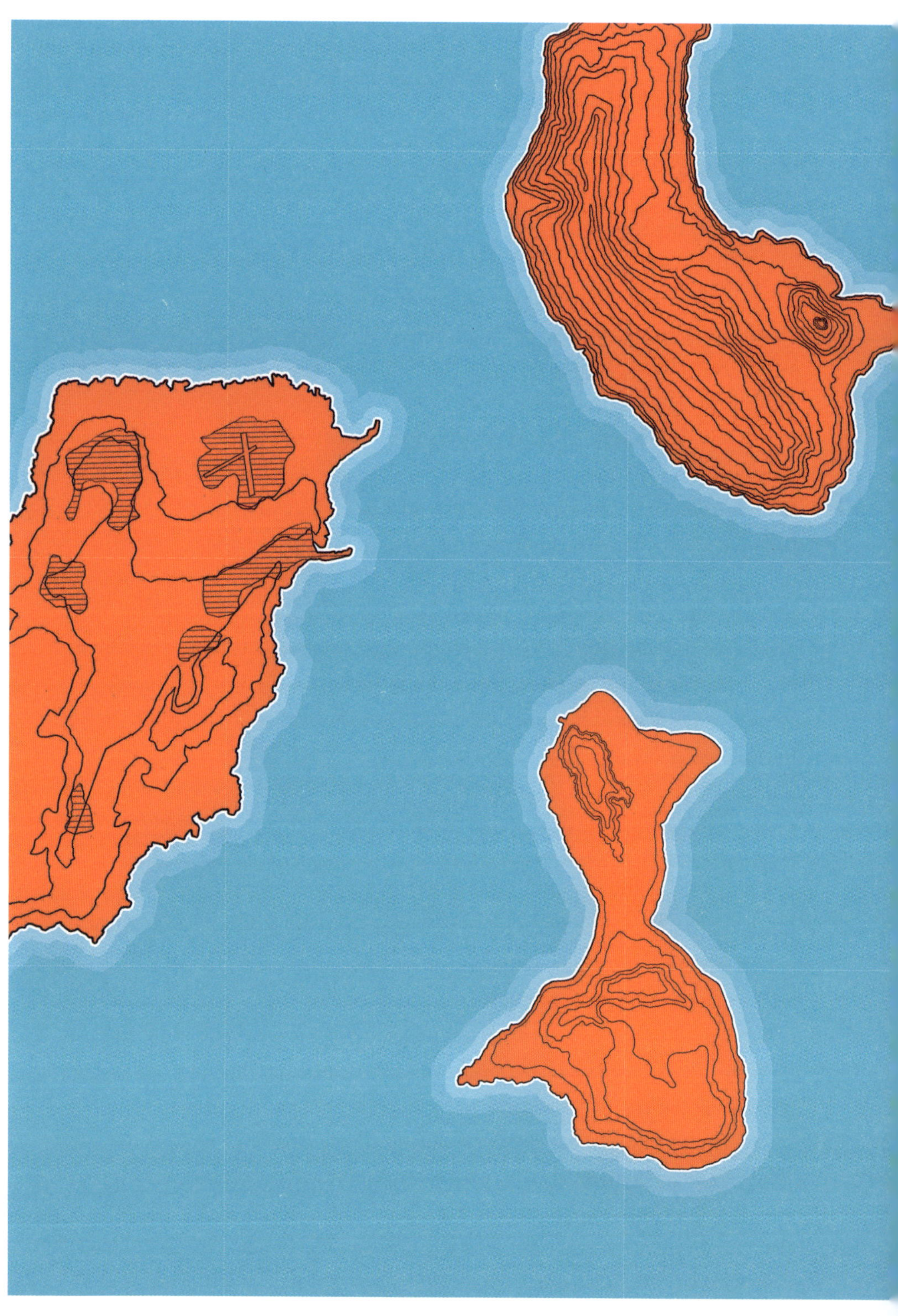

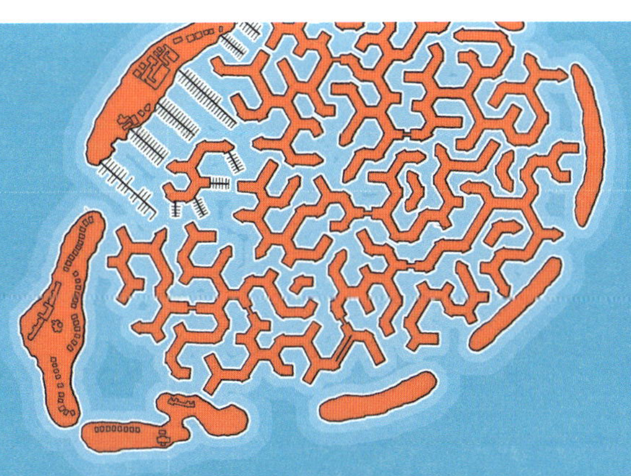

STRANGE ISLANDS

TANA QIRQOS

Sacred Island of the Ark

COUNTRY Ethiopia **AREA** Approximately 12,340m^2 (132,826 ft^2). **POPULATION** Approximately 125. **CHARACTERISTICS** A small rocky island in an Ethiopian lake said to have been the resting place for the Ark of the Covenant, and visited by Mary and the infant Jesus. Today it is inhabited by monks who welcome pilgrims.

ETHIOPIA'S TANA LAKE has twenty-seven holy islands, each with its own history. They are redoubts of the Ethiopian Orthodox church, an ancient branch of Christianity founded in 330 CE. One of the smallest of Tana's islands is its most sacred. This is Tana Qirqos, which is believed to have been the home of the Ark of the Covenant, as well as a stopping place for Mary and Jesus.

The Ark is the holiest of holy objects: it is the box in which the stone tablets inscribed with the Ten Commandments were held. King Solomon built the First Temple in Jerusalem to house the Ark. When the Babylonians sacked Jerusalem and destroyed the Temple, the Ark was lost. Its whereabouts has been a source of legend ever since. For many Christians and Jews, the Ark is the most important physical manifestation of God's presence on Earth. It is especially significant in Ethiopian Christianity. Ethiopian churches are consecrated with a tabot, a little model of the Ark, which is covered up and kept on the altar. Only priests are allowed to see or touch the tabot.

The exclusivity of sacred things is echoed by the exclusivity of holy islands. It seems that anything understood as sacred cannot be *anywhere* ordinary: it has to be beyond ordinary people's profaning gaze. Having remained on Tana Qirqos for, perhaps, 800 years (different accounts give different periods) the Ark moved to its final resting place, the Church of Saint Mary of Zion at Aksum, which is about 280 kilometres (174 miles) northeast of Lake Tana, across the Simien Mountains. Today, only the 'guardian monk' at Aksum may view the Ark. Appointed for life by his predecessor, he spends his life in the chapel of the Ark, never to leave, praying and burning incense.

One of the best accounts of Tana Qirqos is from the travel journalist Paul Raffaele who describes how, on arrival, he was met by 'a barefoot monk clad in a patched yellow robe' who hurried down 'a pathway cut into the rock and peered into our boat'. It is explained that the monk was making sure there were no women aboard. The barefoot monk told Raffaele that women have been 'banned for centuries because the sight of them might fire the young monks' passions'.

The island's monks live in small log huts with conical thatched roofs and their veneration of the Ark is only excelled by another, equally miraculous, story. They can show you the footprints of the Virgin Mary and the child Jesus, as well as the imprint of the Virgin Mary's drapery, all incised into the island's rock. Mary and Jesus are said to have stayed on the island for three months and ten days. Mary felt it was such a wonderful place she didn't want to leave. However, an Angel came to her and told her about the destiny of Jesus and said that she must make the difficult journey back to Egypt and on to Israel.

Raffaele visited the simple shrine where he is told that 'Jesus and Mary sat each day while they were here', but then asks the monk an obvious question, 'What proof do you have that they came here?'. The monk 'looked at me with what appeared to be tender sympathy', writes Raffaele, and replied: 'We don't need proof because it's a fact. The monks here have passed this down for centuries'.

The Ethiopian national saga, the *Kebra Nagast* ('Glory of the Kings'), tells the story of the Ark's arrival. The Queen of Sheba is one of Ethiopia's founding figures and legend tells of her having a child with King Solomon. This child became Emperor Menelik, the first emperor of Ethiopia, and it was he who took the Ark from Solomon's Temple and brought it south, eventually to rest at Tana Qirqos and then Aksum. A line of descent is traced from Sheba to Ethiopia's other monarchs. Haile Selassie was the 225th descendant of Menelik. He was deposed by the military in 1974, bringing the story of Ethiopia's monarchy to an end.

However, Ethiopia's Biblical heritage is still very much alive and both the Old and the New Testament are central to this heritage. The Ark was a Jewish treasure and the monks on Tana Qirqos point to

Jewish ritual artefacts on the island to evidence its presence here. Their proof is found in a small, corrugated metal hut housing a collection of Jewish 'sacrificial stones'. It reveals much about the overlooked nature of Lake Tana, and Tana Qirqos, that the most complete account of the lake's islands and these Jewish stones, remains the one provided by British explorer Robert Ernest Cheesman in a paper published in *The Geographical Journal* in 1935. He wrote that there are three 'stone pillars about 5 feet [about 1.5m] high' and that they were 'sacrificial altars of the Israelite priests; circular basins are cut in the top in which the blood of the victims of sacrifice was caught and thence sprinkled on the people by a priest with a whisk'. Cheesman adds that the altars give 'one of the very few glimpses that have ever been obtained into Ethiopian pre-Christian times'.

The stones, the imprints of holy feet and the location of the Ark are matters of faith rather than science. Archaeologists question their veracity; which implies that they think that Biblical stories can be measured and tested. More fool them. What matters is that generation after generation of monks and devotees have nurtured and passed on these stories. Many of Tana's other islands also have shrines, churches and monasteries and Cheesman again is our best source of detail. He tells us of elderly monks who had not left their sacred spot for fifty years. Such years of devotion are soaked into the stones, here as on every sacred island.

Generations of the devoted, and centuries of murmured prayer, create an aura. Not just prayer but also song. Tana Qirqos is rumoured to be the burial place of Saint Yared, founder of Ethiopia's tradition of sacred music. Saint Yared lived from 505 to 571 CE. He is credited with inventing Ethiopian church music and its unique musical notation system. He also composed Zema, the liturgical chant of the Ethiopian church, as well as delicate seasonal incantations:

Listen to the sound of the footsteps of the rain!
When the rains pour down, the poor rejoice. Listen to the
sound of the footsteps of the rain!

Lake Tana has been a holy site for Ethiopian Christianity for many centuries. Of the lake's other monasteries Daga Estefanos on Daga Island is the most famous. It holds glass cases containing mummified Ethiopian emperors from the thirteenth to seventeenth centuries.

If Lake Tana's holy islands were in Europe or, indeed, if they were anywhere other than Africa, they would be being conserved, catalogued, protected, and would be listed as a World Heritage Site. None of this is happening. Unfortunately, Lake Tana's churches and monasteries are in a rough state and many ancient works of art and precious books have been damaged or stolen. The Ethiopian government has placed Lake Tana on what is called the 'tentative list' for *consideration for nomination* as a World Heritage Site. It has been kicked into the long grass. In the meantime, the pilgrims come, the monks pray, but the holy sites decay. The 2015 announcement of a 'UNESCO Lake Tana Biosphere Reserve' may sound like a step in the right direction. But it's a bit like declaring that the Vatican is worthy of preservation because of the bees and bats that live there. Tana Lake has numerous unique species and its traditional papyrus boats, lumbering hippos and rich birdlife make it a special place. But for believers, this was once the resting place of the Ark, and a site visited by Mary and Jesus. It is one of the world's extraordinary islands.

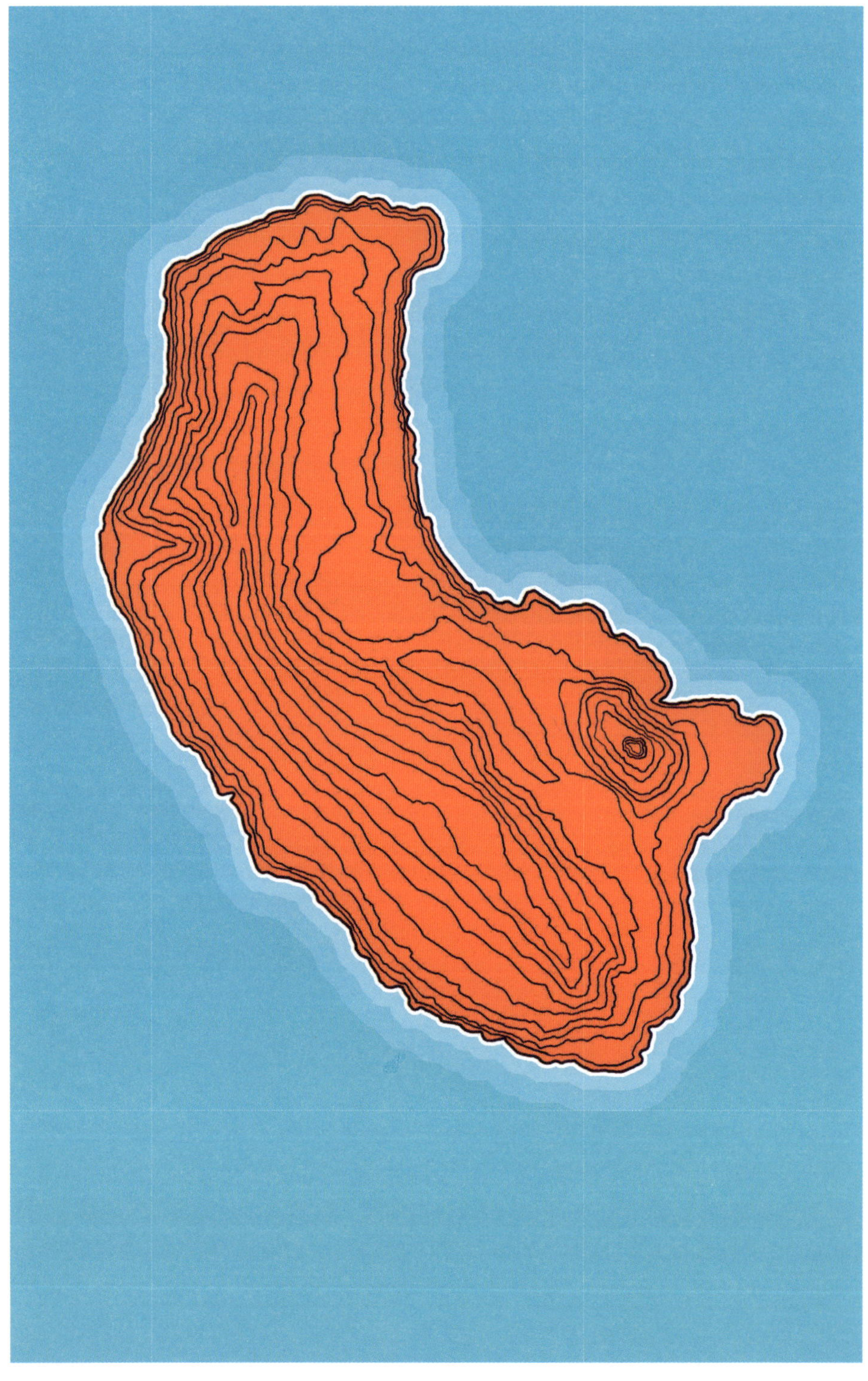

TANNA

'Cargo Cult' Island

COUNTRY Vanuatu **AREA** 550km^2 (210 square miles). **POPULATION** Approximately 30,770. **CHARACTERISTICS** A volcanic island in the South Pacific. It is one of the most traditional islands in the Pacific and famous for its curious 'cargo cults'.

THE ISOLATION OF ISLANDS makes them ideal petri dishes for the incubation of unusual beliefs. Tanna is one of the islands of Vanuatu, an archipelago nation in the western Pacific. It is famous for its so-called 'cargo cults'. 'So-called' because this misleading term suggests that believers are fixated on the hope that 'cargo' will miraculously drop from the sky or wash up on the shore. There is much more to these movements than a desire for free bounty. Nor is the word 'cult' quite right. If we define a cult as a closed and coercive community then these are not cults. Tanna's 'cargo cults' are better described as folk religions and, curious as they are, they rub along and overlap with traditional beliefs as well as the island's dominant faith, Christianity.

Tanna is mountainous and volcanic. For its size – 40 kilometres (25 miles) long and 19 kilometres (12 miles) wide – it's strikingly diverse. Its 31,000 people speak five local languages, each of which has a variety of dialects. Tanna has been inhabited since about 400 BCE and remains one of the most traditional islands in the Pacific. The first European to visit Tanna was James Cook, who arrived in 1774.

The island's new religions are twentieth-century creations. The most important is the John Frum movement. On 15 February, Tanna celebrates John Frum, for believers think this is the date on which he will, one day, return to the island. Men with 'USA' painted in red across their chests and backs parade, holding bamboo rifles. From 1978 the celebration has been accompanied by the raising of an American flag.

Who was John Frum? Accounts differ, but the legend appears to have developed in the 1930s, when a mysterious figure calling himself

John Frum started to appear across the island. Dressed in white trousers, a long-sleeved shirt and a hat with a veil that hid his face, John Frum made promises and prophecies. He would help make the Tannaese as powerful and rich as their white governors. But he also made demands: he asked that people turn back to the old ways. Presbyterian missionaries had succeeded in turning most of Tanna Christian. The old traditions had almost been eradicated, including polygeny, dancing and drinking kava, a root-based tipple popular across the Pacific, which has mildly sedative and euphoric affects and was used to give access to the ancestors. Lamont 'Monty' Lindstrom, an anthropology professor at the University of Tulsa and one of the few foreigners with a thorough knowledge of Tanna, tells us that many of the ancestors' bodies are said to 'lie buried under the island's kava clearings'. Lindstrom recounts that with the 'last mouthful of kava', its drinkers spit into the air, sprinkling kava 'down on these graves, opening up a communication channel. Drinkers mutter prayers and entreaties, and ancestral replies come to them as they sit quietly listening to the kava'.

John Frum proclaimed the coming of a new age. The whites would leave. There would be a return to the way things were. European money should be discarded. People should slaughter their cattle and goats and abandon their gardens and houses. John Frum also foretold that Tanna would literally 'turn over' and become joined to neighbouring islands; that 'mountains would flatten and valleys fill'. John Frum's words, carried by rumour and gossip, found an audience. People did kill their animals and give up farming; some even threw their paper money into the sea. There was a mass exodus from the missionary chapels as well as from schools and plantations, and some followers moved inland where they held traditional feasts and rituals. By May 1941, only a handful of Christian worshippers were left in the island's churches.

Alarmed by this cultural insurrection, the colonial authorities sought to suppress the John Frum movement. The British district agent, and the island's sole colonial authority since 1915, was a man called James Nicol. Like many colonial agents, he appears to have been somewhat out of his depth. He nevertheless arrested two men who he suspected of spreading the new faith, one of whom confessed to dressing

USA

up and pretending to be John Frum. The men were exiled to a distant island but it was too late. By the early 1940s the spirit of John Frum was abroad, and across the island the movement took off. Many more deportations were to follow before Nicol realized that confrontation was counterproductive. The British began to realize that what they were dealing with was not a violent political revolution but something altogether more original – a mystical cultural crusade.

The John Frum movement's interest in 'cargo' and the USA were not its founding principles but developed soon after it emerged and it's easy to see why. During the Second World War thousands of American troops were stationed across the region, bringing with them trucks, planes and supplies of all kinds. These materials fascinated the islanders, many of whom had had little contact with the industrial world. John Frum told a story of how islanders too, one day, might have many of these bright, fascinating things. The characteristic motifs of the movement, including its mock parades, all derive from this time and include red wooden crosses, which began to be erected in fields. This symbol had been seen on the side of US Army ambulances and took on a talismanic quality. US flags, and US military uniforms and insignia, became prized and revered possessions.

The island-wide John Frum Day, still honoured, commenced in 1957 and in the late 1970s the movement's leaders began to involve themselves in national politics. They were critical of plans for the independence of the new nation of Vanuatu because they feared it would auger further intrusions from the outside world and threaten Tanna culture. A John Frum Party was founded to make the nativist case, and in the 1970s its candidate succeeded in getting elected, several times, to a seat to the National Assembly.

In 2007, Chief Isaak Wan Nikiau, the movement's leader, explained that John Frum was 'our God, our Jesus' and that he would return, but the fervour surrounding John Frum has become a shadow of what it was. Missionaries and the encroachment of the commercial world had done what 'John Frum' prophesied and hollowed out much of the uniqueness of Tanna. In 2022, there were fewer than 500 John Frum practitioners, and it is reported that today only one village adheres to the faith.

Even as it dies, the movement continues to evolve. Lindstrom tells us that contemporary adherents have discarded its isolationist tendencies and now believe, or hope, that America will come to Tanna 'to teach people knowledge of how to construct and organize factories to produce the goods they must purchase'. They don't seek cargo, explains Lindstrom, but 'industrial knowledge' so that their island can one day become more than merely a supplier of a raw material (i.e., coconuts) that is processed elsewhere: they would 'vastly prefer to control the entire productive process – a control which would support dignity and their self-vision'.

Tanna's other famous 'cult' is a smaller affair, confined to the village of Yaohnanen. It is known as the centre of the Prince Philip movement, which revered Queen Elizabeth II's husband. This veneration is thought to derive from the conviction that Philip was an incarnation of one of their mountain deities. The villagers believed that Philip would return one day, in spirit form, to his ancestral home. As with the John Frum movement, these are ideas that negotiate between age-old tradition and the confusing yet seemingly all-powerful outside world. Sydney-based anthropologist Kirk Huffman has suggested that following Philip's death, the villagers have probably transferred their adoration to Charles III.

The John Frum and Prince Philip movements may be curious but they are not inexplicable. Each reflects and refracts the profound impact that the twentieth century has had on a small remote island. Tanna's movements take the symbols that come from the impressive but bewildering outside world and co-opt them, gaining some control over them. They have turned powerlessness into agency. They are not 'cargo cults', stupidly looking to the sky, but cultural bridges between the past and a daunting present.

SANTA CRUZ DEL ISLOTE

The Big Horizons of a Crowded Island

COUNTRY Colombia **AREA** Approximately 14,000m^2 (150,695ft^2).
POPULATION Approximately 900. **CHARACTERISTICS** A densely settled fishing community. Its economy is increasingly based on tourism, as the 'world's most crowded island'.

ABOUT NINE HUNDRED people live on this tiny island, often called the most densely populated place in the world. It's a little less than two football pitches in size and 20 kilometres (about 13 miles) off the coast of the South American country of Colombia. From above, it's just a jumble of roof tops, with barely room to insert a cigarette paper between them: a hugger-mugger labyrinth of narrow lanes and ninety-eight houses. It is represented as something of a hellhole, its density associated with poverty and chaos. '"Most crowded place on Earth" where everyone is related has no place for cops or cars', shouts a typical headline, this one from UK's *Daily Star*.

What often gets forgotten about islands is their most obvious quality: they're surrounded by water. That means a large horizon and a big sea, a huge front yard that provides plenty of space to fish, play and travel. 'We are happy,' says local elder Juve Nal, who has lived on the island his whole life. He explains: 'Every day I get to wake up to the sound and the view of the sea. I would not want to live anywhere else'.

For centuries Santa Cruz Del Islote was little known and little visited. Today, it pulls in day-trippers, many of whom never land but gawp from a safe distance. It is a star exhibit for 'extreme geography' click-bait, however, the island's first in-depth study, published in 2023 by Colombian anthropologist Andrea Leiva Espitia, tells a very different story. Leiva Espitia, who lived on the island, called her book

De isla en isla ('From Island to Island'), and its key take-away is in that title. Santa Cruz is not fenced in – its inhabitants are not penned like cattle; the land is crowded but the sea isn't and, in any case, the island is part of an extensive archipelago. The Archipelago of San Bernardo includes the next-door island of Tintipan, which is much larger and covered in lagoons and woodland. The islanders look on their neighbouring islands as part of their domain. One of the fishermen interviewed by Leiva Espitia, Reinaldo de la Hoz, tells his story like this:

> *I spend my time from island to island, I spend my time travelling, I do my duty, I do my job, I work for my children, I work for the ones I love ... One does know where one is born, but one does not know where one dies. I'll die on the islet, because this is where they love me.*

Throughout her interviews, Leiva Espitia discovered that it is not crowds and confinement that define the lives of Santa Cruz, but mobility, the wide-open sea and also, as Reinaldo's words tell us, the bond of family.

The island is pretty much self-run. It's true there are no police but that is because, as another of Leiva Espitia's interviewees tells it, 'There is no crime here,' so 'we do not need them'. In fact, most tiny islands have no police and they are nearly always crime-free. Why? Because on small islands everyone knows everyone else's business. That may sound intrusive but is also means they rarely suffer, or tolerate, the kind of behaviour that, in the view of islanders here as elsewhere, is rampant on the mainland.

Santa Cruzians are also proud of the fact that, in large part, their island was built by them. The island was first occupied in the 1860s but it was too small, so settlers began expanding it with blocks of coral and tree trunks brought from other islands. They created land by burying long wooden poles and making what they call 'corrals', which were then filled in to expand the island. One day, in those early years, the tide delivered something special to the island – a concrete cross.

This miraculous gift from the sea was to give the island its name – Santa Cruz del Islota, or Holy Cross Islet.

Since it has come to global attention, the islanders have found themselves the object of intense curiosity and can feel like they are exhibits in a freak show. Leiva Espitia tells us that there is a 'general discontent caused by being watched by tourists from the boats that anchor off the shore'. She recounts talking with a neighbour when a boat stopped and the on-board tourist guide began his 'usual speech about the living conditions of the people'. On this occasion the guide's patter about how terrible life must be in the 'most crowded place in the world' was interrupted by the neighbour who, tired of hearing the daily spiel, snapped at the surprised tourists: 'That's a lie, it's a lie!'

Santa Cruz is not paradise. Access to fresh water and energy are ongoing problems. The islanders make do with a common cistern, along with domestic ones that store rainwater. For power there is a small generating plant and a solar panel array (apparently paid for by Colombia's Japanese Embassy), which has been built across some of the rooftops. None of these resources is reliable: some days are better than others. The rise of tourism is both curse and cure. Some don't like being stared at but, with the decline of fishing, it's a lifeline. One of the local guides, Adrián Caraballo, explains that tourism is now vital but even he is bothered by the bad habits of some of the island's visitors, especially the piles of rubbish they leave: 'Some tourists are environmentally conscious', he says, 'others not so much'. Waste disposal is not straightforward on Santa Cruz: most of it is ferried to a pit on another island.

The island's biggest challenge is climate change. More frequent and worse storms and sea level rise mean that Santa Cruz is unlikely to see out the century. Alejandro Alzate, a hotel manager on the neighbouring island of Múcura, explains that Santa Cruz experiences regular flooding but the islanders 'won't listen' because 'it means eventually they will have to move'. Alejandro knows the island and understands why its people prefer to avoid thinking about its future: 'Life on Santa Cruz is not something you could find elsewhere. People are proud to live there. It's more than just a community, it's a culture, a way of life. They don't want to be any place else.'

Santa Cruz residents may love their island but its tiny size poses unique challenges. Leiva Espitia explains that islanders have a complex sense of 'the limits between the street and the house, to know where "it is a street" and where "it is a house", and at what times of day one can pass through certain places that, sometimes, are "private"'. She adds that anyone having a bath is 'visible to everyone, even from the patios of some houses'. This is not a place for those who like their privacy. She describes other tricky situations, such as when islanders are trying to use the same space for multiple reasons. For example, the island's only patch of open ground, the Plaza de la Cruz, which is about 15 square metres (around 160 square feet), is where the kids play football, but it is also where adults enjoy socializing. The men who play dominoes in the corners get fed up with being whacked by footballs and younger children complain they have nowhere to play.

Leiva Espitia argues that islanders here have fashioned a distinctive spatial sensibility, which does not so much discard privacy as reimagine it:

> *When one has been living in Santa Cruz del Islote for a long time, the dimensions of space-time change: the alley that seemed small acquires the dimension of a 'street', one learns to ignore listening to the 'private' conversations of one's neighbours and blank them out to avoid conflicts. You know where it is appropriate to pass and where it is not.*

Since there is no room for a cemetery, Santa Cruzians' final journey is across the water, to burial sites on neighbouring islands. It's a fitting end: their island is minute, its streets no more than an arm's length wide, but that does not mean that the islanders' lives are small-scale or to be pitied. Like islanders everywhere they are people of the sea and its many shores.

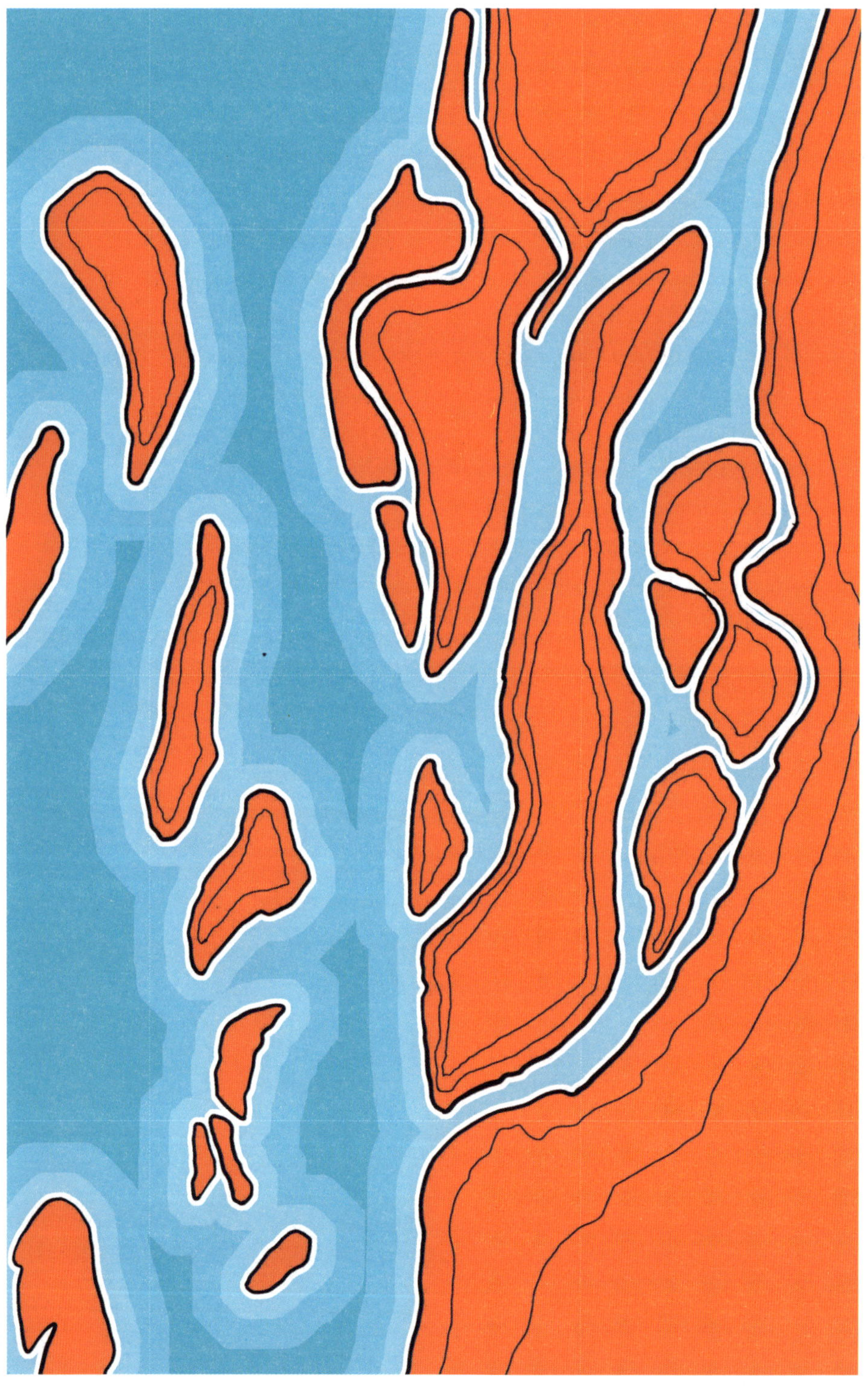

CHARS OF ASSAM

Unsettled Islands

COUNTRY India **AREA** Changeable. **POPULATION** Changeable. **CHARACTERISTICS** Silt islands of the Ganges Delta. Many are farmed and temporarily settled but these islands come and go with the flow of the river.

ACROSS INDIA AND BANGLADESH, thousands of sandy, silty islands wax and wane in the Ganges Delta, appearing and disappearing with the seasons. They offer a shifting, flood-plagued home to millions of farmers and their families. The islands are called chars and they are too mercurial to be properly counted; after each inundation, villagers pick through what is left of their belongings and move to another island.

The Indian state of Assam is tucked in India's northeastern corner and our map shows a few of the chars that you can currently find on a small stretch of the Brahmaputra River. Even though the sea at this point is hundreds of kilometres away, the river is 16 kilometres (nearly 10 miles) wide and sews an intricate pattern between many island farmsteads. The Brahmaputra tumbles from snowy Tibet before it threads its way through Assam and down into Bangladesh, past thousands more chars, where it merges with the Ganges before finding salt water in the Bay of Bengal.

There are around 3,500 chars on the Brahmaputra in Assam. Some are uninhabited but others are tightly packed with little fields growing water-loving crops. Rice and jute are the mainstays of char agriculture, but the rich soil is bountiful, and you'll also find wheat, chilli, maize, peanuts, oilseeds, onions, garlic, sugarcane, peas and much more. Jute is a tall reed-like plant used to make a strong, coarse fabric – 85 per cent of the world's jute supply comes from the Ganges Delta.

All these harvests are at risk of being swept away but creation is as common as destruction; new islands that survive four years or so are deemed ready for new fields and houses. One study of Bangladeshi chars found that 75 per cent of them lasted between one and nine years, while only about 10 per cent lasted for eighteen years or more. Life on the chars is inherently temporary but people stave off the inevitable. They build their homes on the highest land and, if able to, they raise them higher on plinths, giving them a chance of surviving the next inundation.

Living with floods means living with a sense of permanent homelessness. In most of the world, people would think this was intolerable, but on these rivers it's a way of life. The people of the chars have long experience of coping with displacement. One old villager from a char in West Bengal recalls how, back in 1971, 'we lost our homes, land and everything, we had no other option but to migrate and settle on the newly formed Hamidpur Char that emerged in the middle of the river'. Another migration is always around the corner and the same old man adds that after a few years 'when the char was swallowed by the river current, we migrated again'. There is no sense of panic, just resignation: 'These migrations', he explains, 'are now an integral part of our lives and livelihoods'. Unfortunately, it is getting harder: the scale and severity of flooding on the Brahmaputra River is worsening and, since 2012, a series of catastrophic deluges have caused numerous deaths.

A team of Indian researchers found that between the 1970s and 2000s, the people on the chars they studied had to move between four to sixteen times. Despite it being so common, there is a sense of loss each time it happens, perhaps especially among those who see their childhood home swept away. The Indian team talked to a man called Mohammad Rabiul Alam, a primary school teacher, who recalled 'his delightful days on the disappeared land with his big family, including parents, sisters and three brothers'. Since then, they have had to migrate several times, but Mohammad retains a fondness and loyalty for this uncertain, mobile life. The char dwellers adapt in ingenious ways. During floods all routes of communication are severed, so villagers make use of tiny tin boats that they build themselves, which are just big enough for two, and allow them to ferry food and water. If the flood persists, before seeking out a new island, they may

retreat to their rooftops, where they live on food kept safe and dry, stored for just such a day.

In *Dancing with the River*, Kuntala Lahiri-Dutt and Gopa Samanta describe the char dwellers as 'river-gypsies' who are 'citizens of neither one country nor another'. Pushing this idea even further they claim that the 'nomadic' and 'wandering' people of the chars 'inhabit a nonlegal, illegible, ungoverned and ungovernable space'. The chars have only been settled over the past one hundred years or so as waves of migration pushed people across new borders. Many of the Indian char dwellers originally came from Bangladesh, arriving after Partition to occupy empty land. One villager explains that 'no one lived here or used these lands. The char was covered by forest and bushes. We cleared those and started building our houses'. Similar accounts echo across different families' histories. Another old resident tells his story like this:

> *When we, two families, came to this place in 1949 it was not habitable. It was an imposing and vast riverbed covered by bushes and jungles. The jungle was full of snakes, fox, ban beral [wild cats], wild pigs and monkeys. There was not a soul living on these sands. To avoid ending up in the refugee camp, we were moving around in search of land and finally arrived here.*

The islands were empty not only because they were covered in jungle but because they were remote, unstable and making a living from them seemed impossible. Today they support millions of people but the poverty is apparent from a glance at the few public facilities they have. Within the small cross-section of chars in Assam shown on our map there is Uzirar Char High School which, according to a government website, has no classrooms or library, no electricity connection and only one toilet.

The Assamese char dwellers, like those in West Bengal, face a double jeopardy: not only do they live on unstable, ephemeral islands but most are descendants of Muslim settlers from modern Bangladesh.

They have no economic clout and their status in Hindu-majority India is coming under ever greater scrutiny and pressure.

Anindita Chakrabarty, from Mahindra University, tells us that because 'citizenship in India is largely determined by sedentary residence', the Assam char dwellers' legal status, right to residence and ownership of land is 'questioned by the state and a vigilant civil society, entailing doubt and suspicion regularly'. This often culminates, she says, 'in displaced people being labelled illegal foreigners or "Bangladeshis"'. Thus, despite having lived in Assam for generations and speaking Assamese, char dwellers are subject to officially endorsed forms of neglect and even persecution. In 2024 the Assam Chief Minister proclaimed he was on a mission to reclaim the chars from 'encroachers', apparently to safeguard the 'ecological integrity' of the Brahmaputra Valley. According to *The Hindu* newspaper, he also stated that 'the government would start establishing heritage belts and blocks encompassing religious and historic sites where non-indigenous people would not be allowed to acquire land'. The religious sites to be safeguarded are Hindu monasteries and the minister's comments offer a thinly veiled attack on char dwellers because they are Muslim. *The Hindu* reminds its readers that one of the promises of India's ruling party, the BJP led by Prime Minister Narendra Modi, 'is to free large swathes of land belonging to such monasteries from encroachers of "suspect nationality"'.

The waxing and waning of these islands is reflected in the coming and going of the rights and status of the people who live there. In Assam, as in West Bengal, many can trace their roots to farmers from Bangladesh who began cultivating land that no one else wanted. As India has become more religiously polarized, and its government has pursued a religiously partisan agenda, the people of its river islands have come to be cast as permanent outsiders. The future of the chars was always uncertain. Today this uncertainty is compounded: the challenges of farming a transient landscape have become mixed up with the challenges of living in a country where non-Hindus are cast as usurpers.

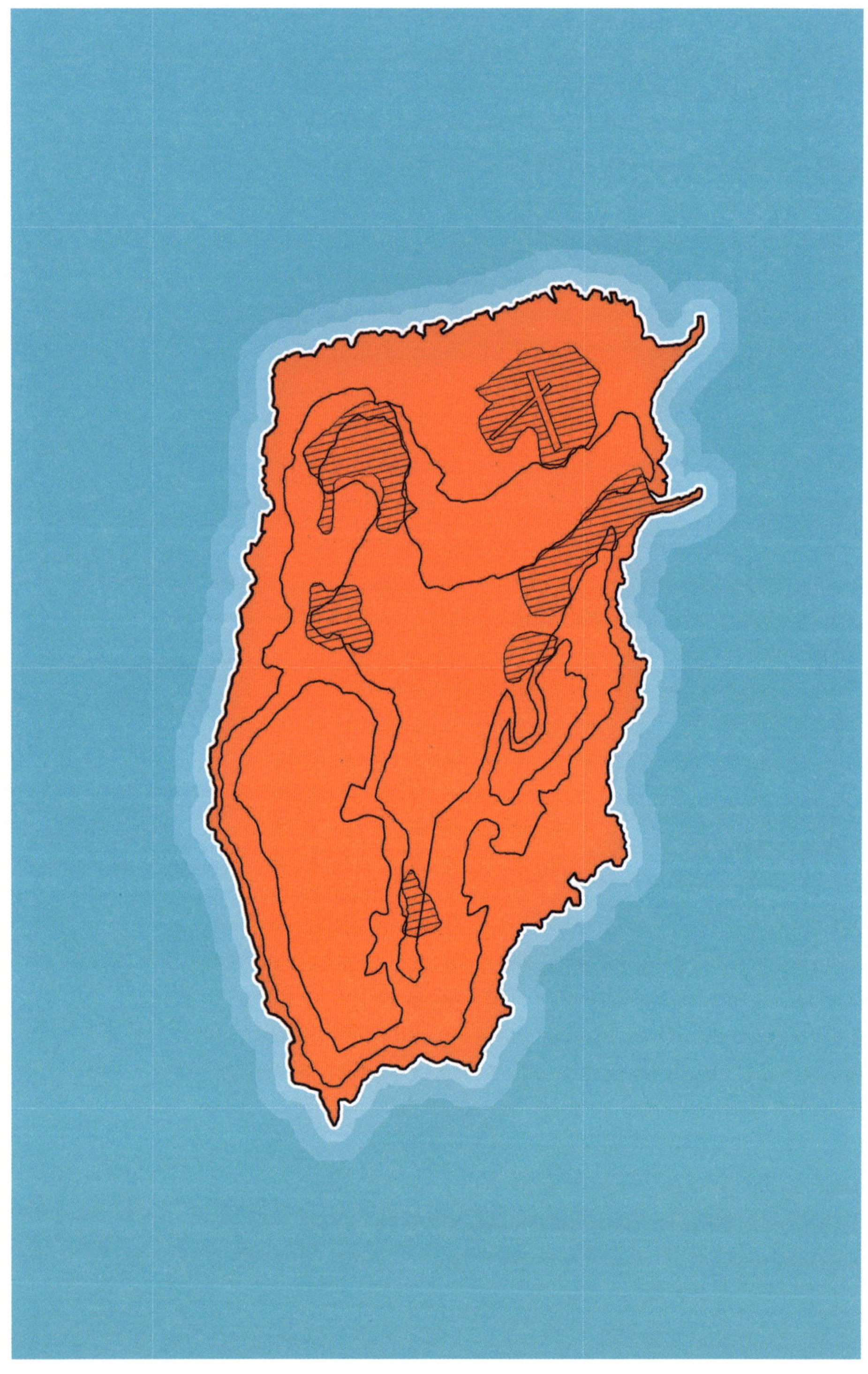

KIHNU

Island of Women

COUNTRY Estonia **AREA** 16.4km^2 (6.3 square miles). **POPULATION** Approximately 700. **CHARACTERISTICS** A tranquil island in the Gulf of Riga known for its unique cultural traditions, which include music, costume and the prominent and powerful role of women.

SMALL ISLANDS KEEP hold of traditions. They are often conservative places. However, there's a paradox here: many of the world's traditions do not fit easily into modern definitions of what being conservative means. Gender roles are a good example. The conservative idea that women should just cook, sew and be submissive doesn't play well on small islands where everyone has to contribute to whatever needs doing. The very traditional island of Kihnu, just off the coast of Estonia and famed for its peasant costumes, unique songs and dances as well as its smoked seal delicacies, is also famous for its multi-tasking women.

Kihnu is an island of fields and patches of woodland some 10 kilometres (6.2 miles) distant from the mainland and encompasses just 16.4 square kilometres (6.3 square miles). The island is home to several hundred people in four villages. In years past, most of the men were fishermen and seal hunters, often away for long periods. Today the economy relies on tourists drawn here by its unique, old-fashioned character but also by headlines like 'What life is like on the island run by women' and 'Kihnu: Europe's last surviving matriarchy'.

Looking closer – it seems that while Kihnu has a distinctive tradition of women taking on public roles, the notion that it is a 'matriarchy' is misleading. Rather this is a claim used to sell the island to tourists. The truth is that women don't rule Kihnu, but they do run its farms and perform certain key rites of passage like weddings and funerals. Men are not marginalized, crushed or pushed aside (as women are in patriarchal societies) but women have a central and visible role.

Weddings are the most important ceremonies on the island and they are highly ritualistic. It is the bride's mother who gives permission for the wedding procession to come and get the bride, and sends her away. It is the groom's mother who welcomes the bride at the door of her new home and ritually removes her existing headdress and, according to the Estonian anthropologist Ingrid Rüütel, 'sets a special coif on her head and puts the apron over her skirt, which are both marks of a married woman'. The wedding singers, all women, play an important role too; one wedding choir from the bride's side and one from the groom's. These church events are presided over by women, which reflects the fact that on Kihnu men do not regularly attend church; they come for special occasions but church is a female-dominated institution.

The Norwegian photographer Anne Helene Gjelstad has made a study of the Kihnu women and their bright traditional costumes. Having got to know the islanders, she explains that being married is the key to a woman's status. 'It was very hard on the women who didn't find a man, who didn't get married and didn't have children,' she says, adding that such women 'were not considered as valuable as the other women'. Gjelstad's photographs of women on Kihnu capture both a traditional and a unique culture; it is a place of sisterhood, and of strong, capable women, but they are not images of a feminist paradise.

The mixture of conservatism and what an outsider – noting that women have public and central roles – might mistake for matriarchy, is clear from the importance accorded to marriage but also from how land ownership and control works on the island. Farms on Kihnu are divided between sons. Since men were so often away it has meant widows or wives have had to act as managers and overseers of farmsteads. In terms of land ownership Kihnu is a patriarchy, but its farms are run by women.

Small islands can defy expectations and assumptions. Kihnu is a socially conservative island, but women are prominent and often dominant in both the private and public sphere. The absence of men is striking. One resident, when asked how many of the island's year-round residents are men, suggests 'maybe five', though *The New York*

Times journalist who asked the question in 2019 could find only two – 'a visiting documentary filmmaker and a builder fixing a house'. An islander explained that 'we have totally different mentalities than people on the mainland'. Yet this American reporter found that the idea of feminism was 'met with bewilderment here. The reasoning: Of course, women are capable. Of course, women are competent. But no, men and women aren't equal – women have proven they can do everything men can, but men can't do everything women can'.

The central role of women goes beyond running farms, households and businesses. Women are also central to the most famous of the island's cultural traditions – its music. The island has been declared a 'Masterpiece of the Oral and Intangible Heritage of Humanity' by UNESCO. The awarding statement from UNESCO talks about the island's unique 'oral tradition of pre-Christian origin, known as runic or Kalevala-metre songs'. The music of the island is nationally famous, and Estonia's most popular folk singer, Kihnu Virve, was from the island. Born in 1928 she lived in a log cabin on Kihnu till her death in 2022 and from the age of fifteen composed songs about life, labour and love.

Younger generations of female singers and dancers have kept the island's ancient musical traditions alive and today teach them to the children on the island's school and in its civic centre.

Kihnu is increasingly a tourist island, and the survival of its traditions is far from certain. The population is ageing and young people are moving away. A few decades ago it looked inevitable that the uniqueness of the island – its songs, dances, costumes and food, as well as the distinct prominence of its women – would not make it into the current century. Some thought a traditional wedding in 1994 would be the last. However, perhaps in response to the fact that so many outsiders find value in these traditions, local people have begun to rediscover them. The 2010s saw several traditional weddings and Ingrid Rüütel tells us that they have acted to 'strengthen solidarity and identity'. Tourists are a paradoxical presence: they weaken tradition but also strengthen it. They hollow it out by turning it into a cliché, but they want to buy it – the craft objects, the costumes, the music – and, hence, give it monetary value. Is the traditional culture of Kihnu turning into a performance? Perhaps. But in the modern world, that is the way 'traditional culture' survives. After all, the islanders are just like you and me: modern people who welcome affirmation and celebration, especially if it comes with an income stream.

In a twist to this story, the twenty-first century is seeing men increasingly wanting their role in Kihnu's culture to come out of the shadows. In 2009 the Kihnu Sea Association was founded to collect seafaring stories and revive men's traditional handicrafts. Kihnu men have also started playing traditional instruments. The vocal and instrumental ensemble Kihnu Poisid (Kihnu Boys) is now popular all over Estonia. The 'island of women' is not fixed in time nor an amusing redemptive mirror for patriarchy. It is changing and a new phase may be starting – a new era in which island men begin to emulate island women, and take on the pleasures, burdens and rewards of 'traditional culture'.

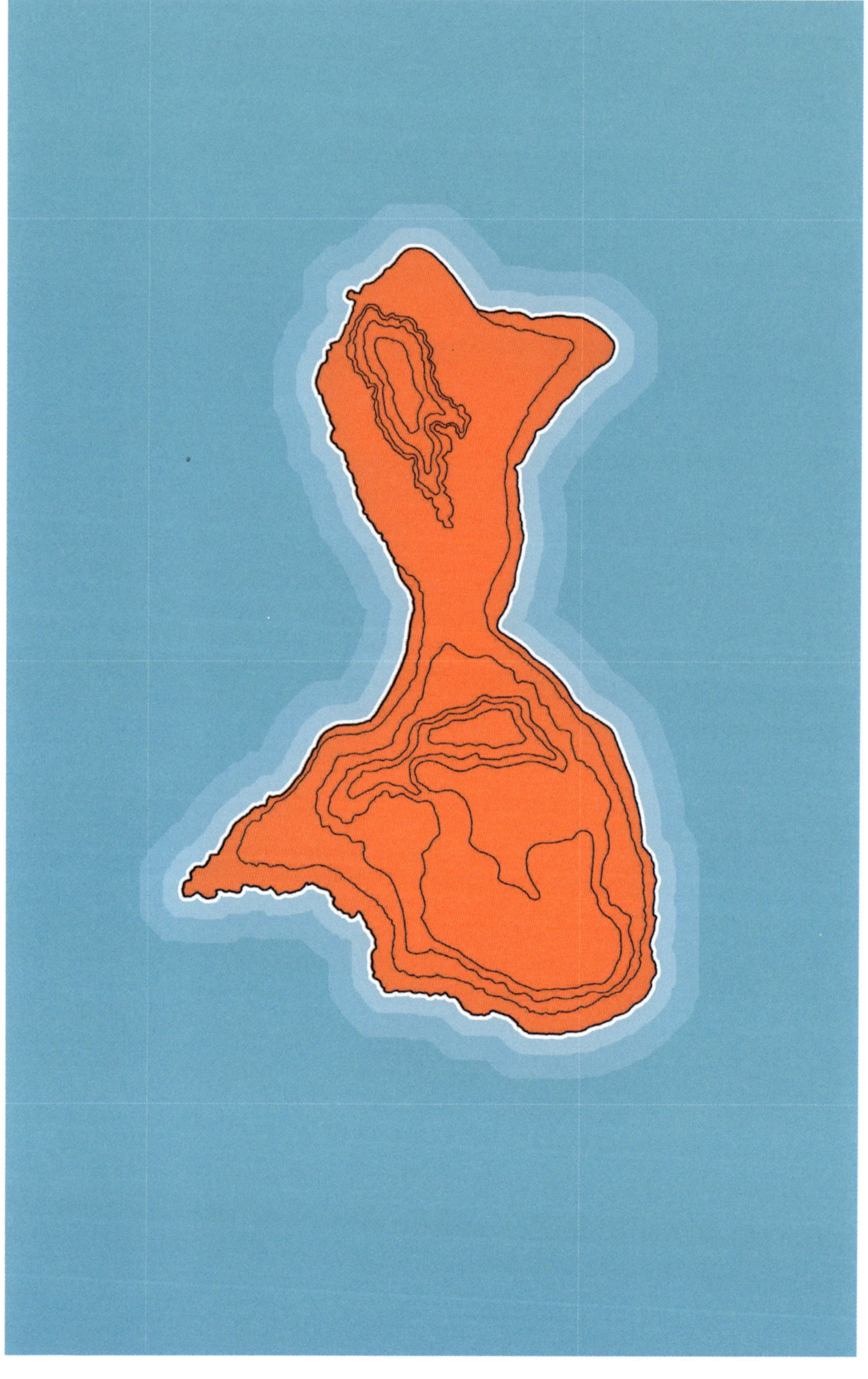

SAMSON

An Island Back in Time

COUNTRY United Kingdom **AREA** Approximately 0.52km² (0.2 square miles). **POPULATION** Zero. **CHARACTERISTICS** Today the largest uninhabited island of the Isles of Scilly, but with a long and tragic history of human settlement.

THE PEOPLE OF SAMSON were the last in England to keep faith with the Old Calendar. In 1582 Pope Gregory decreed that the Julian calendar, which had been used for 600 years, was no longer fit for purpose. A new, more accurate, Gregorian calendar was introduced and, as a result, Christmas and New Year were shunted forward by almost two weeks. It was a sensible reform – now the number of days aligned with the solar year – but islands are often stubbornly resistant to sensible reform. The Old Calendar prevailed on Samson right up to 1855, when its people were dragged from their homes and the island forcibly emptied. The last to go was a woman with a trick up her sleeve. Ann Webber is said to have put a spell on the overseer, as he ordered her to the boat. It is recorded that 'his legs would not move, he was unable to get back into his boat, and the Tresco boatmen had to persuade the lady to lift her enchantment'.

Samson is an hourglass-shaped island with a low-lying hill at either end, each dotted with prehistoric cairns. It is the largest of the uninhabited islands of the Scillies, a cluster of 200 or so islets and islands, 43 kilometres (27 miles) west of England's western tip. The best chronicle of the Scillies' lost past is *Exploration of a Drowned Landscape* by Charles Thomas. The book's title reflects the fact that before the Scillies there was Ennor, Cornish for 'The Land'. Ennor was a big island whose higher peaks are now the main islands of Scilly. Ennor was always shrinking but everywhere you look on the Scillies you can see its phantom traces – nowhere more so than on Samson, whose hills, shores and waters are all scattered with the stone remnants of ancient lives and deaths. Thomas devotes a chapter to Samson and is clearly taken with the place: 'here virtually frozen since 1855, is the setting of a 4,000-year interaction between man, the animal and vegetable kingdoms, the rocks and the land, and the steadily encroaching sea.'

The story of Samson is a tale of hard lives and meagre rewards. Islands that have known umpteen generations but are now abandoned have a powerful character. Their soil and stones have long been worked and known. Yet all that remains are roofless rooms and the groan of wind and waves. Many writers and poets, such as the Cornish poet Geoffrey Grigson, writing in 1946, capture the melancholy of Samson.

Local legend says that Samson was once the bastion to two lawless families, the Webbers and the Woodcocks, who were descended from shipwrecked privateers. A tragedy, so the story goes, overwhelmed both families. During the Napoleonic Wars nineteen men and boys from Samson boarded and commandeered a French ship that had sailed close by. The reward for their daring was to be ordered to sail the ship, complete with enemy crew, to the mainland. Near Wolf Rock, which today bears a stout lighthouse, the ship was holed and went down along with all aboard. Charles Thomas is doubtful about aspects of this tale and disputes the idea that the islanders were brigands. Evidence of what life was like on Samson is scarce, but Thomas tells us that inhabitants were likely to have been more pious than piratical. They were hardworking, Bible-fearing but starvingly poor. The harsh and treeless island they lived on did not provide for plenty.

Samson gets its name from an ancient Welsh saint, Samson of Dol, but it has had less poetic names. Rat Island was one. The sixteenth-century travel writer John Leland wrote: 'Ther is one isle of the Scylleys cawled Rat Isle, [on] which be so many rattes that [no] horse, or any other lyvyng best be browght thyther they devor hym.'

One of the best descriptions we have of life on this remote island comes from 1818, and the observer who wrote this down was 'Bo'sun' Smith, a Baptist minister from the mainland. He toured the inhabited off-islands of the Scillies and found Samson to be the most wretched: 'They ask only for the means of obtaining just sufficient bread and potatoes to keep them alive,' he wrote, adding that the 'families are very poor, and have suffered much distress; their chief support has

been limpets, as the immense piles of empty shells before their doors sufficiently testify'.

To this day, mounds of limpet shells – long seen as a 'famine food' for coastal people in Britain – can be found close-by the islanders' collapsed stone dwellings. Food was just one of the challenges they faced. Another was water. Samson has no spring, so a long tiresome boat journey had to be made to fetch fresh water in barrels. Another problem was fuel. Peat had been dug away from the hills and the supply of driftwood was irregular. An 1841 visitor tells us that the islanders used dried seaweed. It was plentiful but there are good reasons it is a fuel of last resort: it is hard to keep dry and produces a nasty acrid smell when burnt.

In 1834 the Scillies got a new Lord Proprietor, Augustus Smith, and it was he who decided that Samson should be emptied. Once he had achieved this, Smith turned the island into his private deer park. The deer didn't last, with many attempting to swim to better ground. The motive for Smith's eviction appears not to have been greed but a dislike of what Samson embodied: poverty. I suspect, even more galling for Smith, was Samson's medieval irrationality, as seen in its zany patchwork of tiny farming plots. These allotment-sized strips were the opposite of everything the modern, reform-minded Lord Proprietor thought he represented. He was legally able to order the islanders off because, ironically, given Smith's distaste for backwardness, his power was feudal and absolute.

Then as now, Samson (like most of the Scillies) is owned by the Royal Family, in the form of the Duchy of Cornwall. In 1847, not many years before it was emptied, Samson had a pair of royal visitors, Prince Albert, husband of Queen Victoria, and his son, the future 'playboy King', who was to become King Edward VII. Apparently the little prince captured a fledgling black-backed gull, which Charles Thomas relishes telling us would have been 'capable of giving his chubby fingers a very much harder nip than anything he might expect from his theatrical lady-friends in later life'. Thomas adds that 'No doubt the islanders stared, bewildered, at their courteous German visitor. One wonders what he made of the omnipresent limpet-shell middens.'

I want to hand the last words of Samson's story to Charles Thomas. He loved this lonely island and, reciting the names of the Samson families and the names they gave their little lanes and fields, his account of the afterlife of Samson somehow gives voice to the many, empty, silent islands across the world where, once, generations of people lived and worked.

On the deserted island the autumn gales would strip the thatches, men would come to remove the rafters, and the walls begin to crumble, until nothing save the great piles of limpet-shells, the forlorn little homes and the ruined hearths would be left amid the encroaching bracken in Old Lay and Up-and-Down Field and Back-of-the-Hill [and] with each returning spring, primroses that bygone Weber and Woodcock hands had planted. Within such a sadness, even the most sympathetic enquirer must be conscious of creating an intrusion; and among all those strange nuances of atmosphere that Samson still breathes, grief is perhaps the strongest.

OCEAN FLOWER

A Modern Fairy Tale

COUNTRY People's Republic of China **AREA** 8km^2 (3 square miles). **POPULATION** Estimates suggest above 100,000. **CHARACTERISTICS** A large and elaborate artificial island off the coast of Hainan; a mixed leisure and residential development, part of a flotilla of extravagantly-shaped Chinese holiday islands.

THIS IS A STORY about a fairy tale kingdom. It is also a story about money. And about modern China: its rise and its love affair with real estate.

Ocean Flower is the world's largest and most spectacular artificial island. Built just off the coast of the island of Hainan, China's most southerly province, it is shaped like a lotus blossom, with a petalled flower head in the middle and leaves scrolling west and east. Its central spaces feature a medieval castle, artificial mountains, streets of mock European buildings as well as pagodas and mosque-like temples, all swirled round with funfair train lines, lakes and roller coasters. It is truly bonkers.

One favourite destination is Wedding Manor, which an excitable press blurb describes as a place where couples 'can have a romantic date ... to stimulate the hormones of love'. Beyond the Wedding Manor you can find a 'dreamy European castle', from which it is an easy stroll through eating and shopping streets designed as fantasy visions of Russia, the USA, the Black Forest, the Mediterranean and different regions of China. These eye-popping, brightly painted townscapes are flanked by two connected islands that are covered in rows of waterfront tower blocks, originally designed to accommodate 200,000 residents.

It's vast. Yet Ocean Flower is only one of many artificial islands that are, or were until recently, taking shape off the island of Hainan, a Chinese province that is slightly smaller than Taiwan. Ocean Flower has been especially controversial. The Beijing government demanded the demolition of thirty-nine of Ocean Flower's high-rise towers, citing environmental and construction problems and the developer, China Evergrande, having racked up an extraordinary $300 billion in debt, became the world's most indebted property developer. In 2024, after it was unable to offer a convincing restructuring plan, the company was declared bankrupt.

Ocean Flower is high risk, high stakes and crisis-ridden, yet it's a survivor. It opened in 2020 and continues to welcome millions of visitors, nearly all from mainland China. On Chinese review sites, there is a lot of enthusiasm, especially about the visitor attractions, which are often called 'dream-like' and extraordinary. There are critical appraisals too, but these are focused on the island's residential blocks and reviews also mention that the island has a lot of 'intense construction', with many unfinished attractions. Yet all this activity seems only to whet appetites, particularly for the emerging streets that are based on 'Arabian fairy tales', and which beckon with 'oriental elements and colours, with a mysterious and intense Islamic style'.

Short-stay trippers are enjoying Ocean Flower. But it was not supposed to be just a funfair: it was also designed as a place to live, with a large permanent population. It's here that things don't look quite so fairy tale. On the Chinese messaging and social media site WeChat, users have reported that there are problems 'such as the concrete protective layer falling off and steel bars rusting in the underground garage'. Local radio has aired complaints of 'cracked columns, falling cement and severe rust of steel bars'. Follow-up comments vent frustration and anger.

The tycoon behind Ocean Flower and founder of Evergrande is Hui Ka Yan, once one the wealthiest men in the world. Hui was the pin-up boy of rags to riches China: he showed that hard work and savvy business skills could take you to the top. Evergrande's business model was to borrow huge sums of money, commission projects and then start selling apartments, irrespective of their likely completion. The buyers shouldered the risk and the company earned a fortune. For a while it worked. Hui became a legend and he entered the inner circle of Communist Party advisors. A photograph of him at a Party conference wearing a belt with a garish 'H' Hermès gold buckle went viral on social

media in 2012. Hui was called the 'belt brother'. With his penchant for large yachts and private jets Hui became the face of the new China. His flamboyance was his downfall. It made him a useful political target. Unfortunately for Hui, President Xi decided his premiership was going to turn the page on excessive displays of private riches. Suddenly Hui and his company were in the political crosshairs. Hui's net worth stood at $45.3 billion in 2017 but, after the liquidation of Evergrande and subsequent fire sales, by October 2023 it had tumbled to $979 million. Hui was taken away by police and placed under 'residential surveillance'.

The story of Ocean Flower is not having a happily-ever-after ending but nor is it a simple lesson in 'decline and fall'. Too much money has been spent to pull the plug. Hainan's provincial government, based in the capital of Haikou, is pursuing a tourism and real-estate-led development strategy, and it needs Ocean Flower to succeed. In the early years of this century, it granted permission for the construction of a lot of artificial islands. Some have an uncertain fate but others are doing well. Phoenix Island off Hainan's south coast, whose pod-like towers pulse with multicoloured patterns, has been welcoming holidaymakers since 2015. Although at time of writing it's only half built, another likely success story is the twin islands of Sun Moon Bay, one shaped like the Sun, the other a crescent moon.

Other new islands have turned out to be disasters. Just off the shores of the regional capital, Haikou, you would once have seen 'gourd island', or Huludao. It was a new island with bulbous ends and a thin midriff and the master plan revealed swirling, sail-shaped buildings and a huge central tower that was going to feature 'ultrastar hotels'. None of this came to pass. Scraggy bushes soon began to colonize its empty sands and then the order came for it to be demolished. The island was scooped away, vanished from the map.

The story of Hainan's islands isn't just about Ocean Flower or about one developer getting greedy. It's also about the tussle between central and regional governments: Beijing and Haikou. In China, displays of regional independence often result in pushback from the centre. The enthusiasm that the central authorities have found for clamping down on breaches of 'environmental standards' on Hainan's new islands is as much about politics as it is about ecological protection.

Yet Ocean Flower won't be halted and the same can be said for Phoenix Island and the Sun and Moon islands. They have become too big to fail. Execution has also been stayed on a clutch of other artificial holiday islands, whose fate remains unclear. One such is Nanhai Pearl Island, shaped into a yin-yang symbol. The 'yin' half is supposed to become a residential complex and the 'yang' a marina. The base of the island has been built but little else.

Island-building on Hainan is a turbulent and unpredictable business: islands are announced, fantastical plans are drawn up, and sometimes the end result is jaw-droppingly spectacular; other times, it turns to scrubland and a quiet death. However, there is good reason to suspect that, on balance, the former destination is the more likely than the latter. The major industry in Hainan is now real estate. You might think that building islands was an expensive way of creating a visitor attraction or selling property but, in fact, because the price of urban land is so high, it works out to be a cheap option. It can be ten times more expensive to buy land onshore than to build in the sea. Moreover, in China all city land is owned by the state. This also explains why entrepreneurs are tempted to go offshore. The sea is open to unfettered capitalism in a way other places are not.

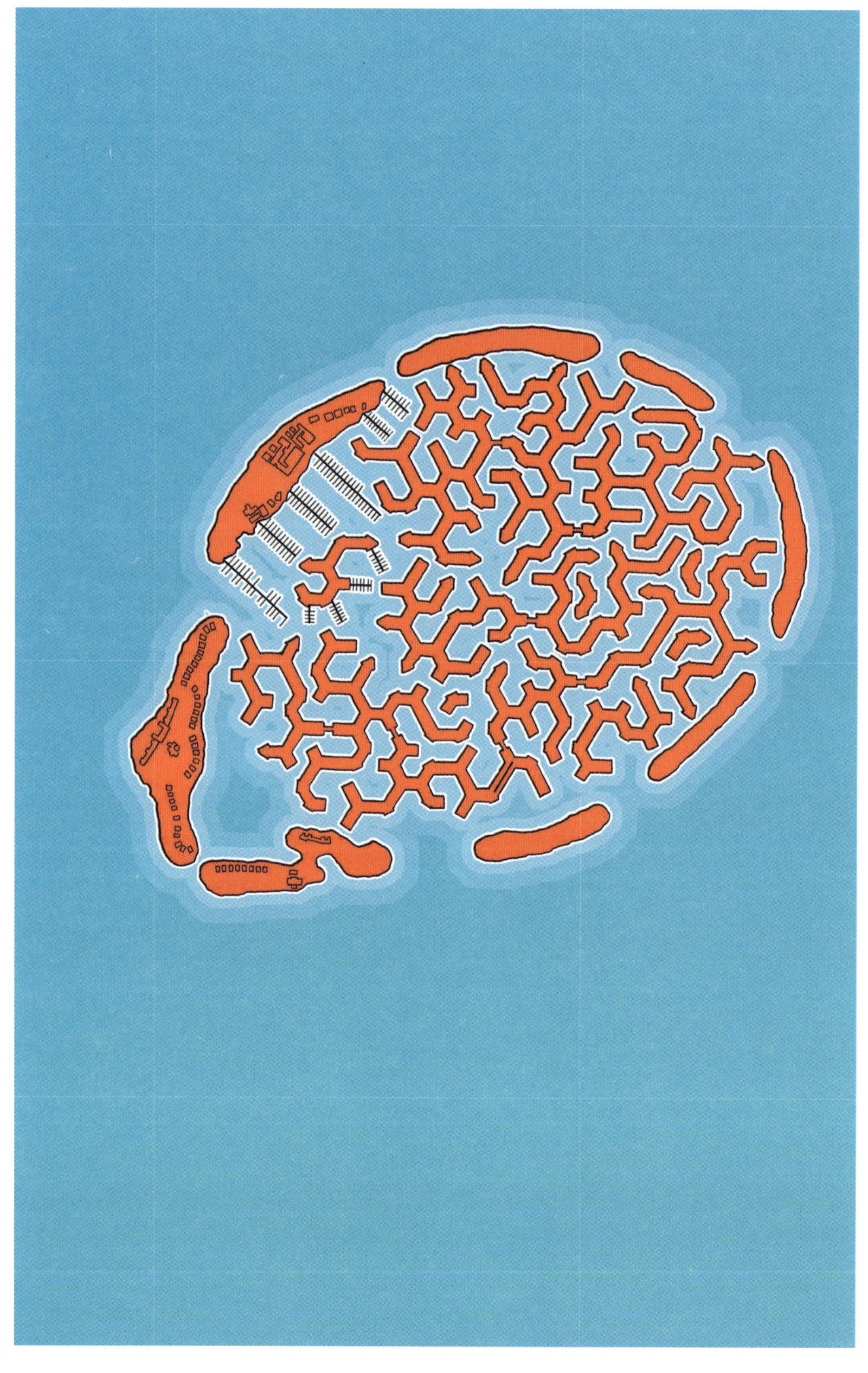

MALDIVES FLOATING CITY

Islands of the Future?

COUNTRY Maldives **AREA** To be confirmed. Under construction at time of writing. **POPULATION** Zero. The projected population is 20,000. **CHARACTERISTICS** An ambitious network of floating structures – under construction – which are designed to be safe from the rising sea levels that threaten the rest of the Maldives.

MALDIVES FLOATING CITY is the most exciting of many new schemes that signpost a new relationship with water as sea levels rise. Its first colourful modules were towed into place in 2023, with the idea that they link and lock into a coral-shaped townscape, a buoyant jigsaw of houses, shops and businesses that is both resilient and beautiful.

People have been living on floating structures for thousands of years and, over the past few decades, dozens of floating communities have been spawned on rivers, lakes and bays. There are over twenty in the Netherlands alone. This plan for the Maldives takes an existing and tested practice to the next level. It's a stand-alone settlement in a 2-square-kilometre (0.77-square-mile) lagoon, a 15-minute boat ride from the capital, Malé, and designed to be a distinct, separate place rather than an add-on to somewhere else.

Due to open in the late 2020s, it follows decades of island building in the Maldives. Many are for tourists but the biggest is for ordinary Maldivians and is called Hulhumalé, but also the 'City of Youth' and the 'City of Hope'. As long as sea levels don't rise too high, Hulhumalé should be able to accommodate about half the country's population. Well away from tourists is another extraordinary island, Thilafushi: an artificial island built for dusty, dirty industries like cement packing but also to receive the huge quantities of rubbish generated by catering to so many big-spending visitors. Critics have long pointed out that these islands, constructed on top of coral reefs, harm sea life and that the Maldives can't keep pushing nature aside if it wants a long-term future. While most new artificial islands destroy the marine environment, the hope is that the Floating City will enhance it: new corals will be planted on the underside of the buildings and existing reefs will be left unmolested.

The Maldives lies in the middle of the Indian Ocean and sells itself as a natural paradise. In fact it's one of the most artificial places on the planet. Hulhumalé, and other vital islands, have been won from the sea and raised to make them less vulnerable to surges and storms. Constructed islands of all sorts, catering for the nearly two million tourists who come each year, freckle the country's warm waters. Despite all this activity, most of the archipelago's 1,190 islands are less than 1 metre (3 feet) above the water and, since sea level is likely to top this towards the end of the century, the Maldives is facing an uncertain future.

The vision of a floating city emerged after a headline-grabbing stunt. When President Mohamed Nasheed held a cabinet meeting underwater in 2009, with ministers in scuba gear, it was a media sensation, providing surreal yet iconic images of a global threat. The one European country that is on the same page as the Maldives is the Netherlands, which has long battled the sea. They wasted no time in connecting President Nasheed to Waterstudio, a Dutch company that specializes in floating buildings. Waterstudio's bold response was the Floating City. It quickly met with Nasheed's approval: he declared that 'In the Maldives, we cannot stop the waves, but we can rise with them'. The Floating City goes up and down with the water level but it is also designed to be stable, even in bad weather. The projected population is 20,000 living in 5,000 brightly painted sea-facing houses and set in shallow, crystal-clear waters.

The design plans make the Floating City look gorgeous. But in a country where foreign money often calls the tune, the question of who is going to live in the Floating City is going to be controversial. The designers, developers and the Maldivian government suggest that the

project will be as much for locals – what the developers call 'local fishing families who, for centuries, have called the area home' – as incomers. A 2021 press release states that prices will start from $250,000 for a family home. While that might sound inexpensive to international buyers, with the average income in the Maldives being a little over $11,000 per annum, those prices don't look geared to 'local fishing families'.

The story of the Maldives Floating City is as much about the Netherlands, where it was drawn up, as it is about the Maldives. The Netherlands has a unique place in the unfolding story of living with water. One name has emerged as a central character in the latest chapter in this story – Koen Olthuis, the director of Waterstudio. Born in 1971 this lanky, artfully dishevelled Dutchman is a busy global leader in the floating cities movement. Olthuis has a vision of modular, slot-in marine communities and many of the schemes he has been involved in, such as the Floating Houses moored off the artificial islands of IJburg in Amsterdam, have already proved successful. Floating structures are opening up a new conversation about the mobility of buildings. Buildings on land are rigid and immoveable. They can't swim so many will sink. In fast-changing, flood-prone and drowning landscapes such as the Maldives this is a problem. Floating structures are part of the solution: they can rise up and survive floods but they can also be moved far away, or just round the corner; somewhere out of harm's way.

Olthuis has written a book-length manifesto with another architect, David Keuning, called *Float! Building on Water to Combat Urban Congestion and Climate Change*. It makes a vigorous case for almost anything and everything being better on water. We should start, Olthius and Keuning tell us, with 'relocating functions that take up a lot of space but have low economic value'. They call this 'trading places' and it means putting things like parks, greenhouses, refineries and golf courses on water. Critics like to point out that floating structures won't last without continuous maintenance; that they are only for the rich; and that they cannot be upscaled for the masses. Each of these points has merit and each requires a response but when they are used to dismiss the whole idea of floating structures they are shortsighted. Sea levels are rising, coasts are eroding and populations are growing. Unless we favour abandoning coastal and riverside cities, new, attractive and workable ideas such as floating buildings are certainly going to be needed.

Floating structures have been up and running for decades and they are highly adaptable. In terms of range of uses, Japan has the most impressive examples: they include a floating airport runway, floating bridges, a floating solar power station and a floating oil storage base. More recently the world's largest floating fish farm was ferried from China to Norway. In the Netherlands, Rotterdam has a floating dairy farm, with rainwater captured on the roof and floating solar panels used to supply energy. Another Dutch flagship innovation is the Schoonschip, a trendy, individualistic floating neighbourhood in the Buiksloterham district of Amsterdam, which uses canal-based heat pumps, along with solar, to heat its homes.

There are other floating communities in the offing. Urban Rigger is a new floating neighbourhood in an unused harbour space in Copenhagen. A collaboration between the United Nations and marine innovators Oceanix is promising a South Korean venture currently called Oceanix Busan. Like the Maldives plan, the idea is that modular platforms will be towed into place and linked together, though the South Korean scheme is even more ambitious: it is hoped this floating city could be home to as many as 150,000.

There is a lot of excitement in the world of floating cities. We are just at the beginning of the story. It remains a thrill ride, and appeals to adventurous, well-heeled people who care about the planet. Will it save the world? Of course not. I doubt that these new islands will ever accommodate tens or hundreds of millions of people. It's not a panacea. But anyone who dismisses it should take a look at the other options. Doing nothing isn't one of them. As part of the mix of fixes that will help us navigate the next two centuries, floating cities are here to stay.

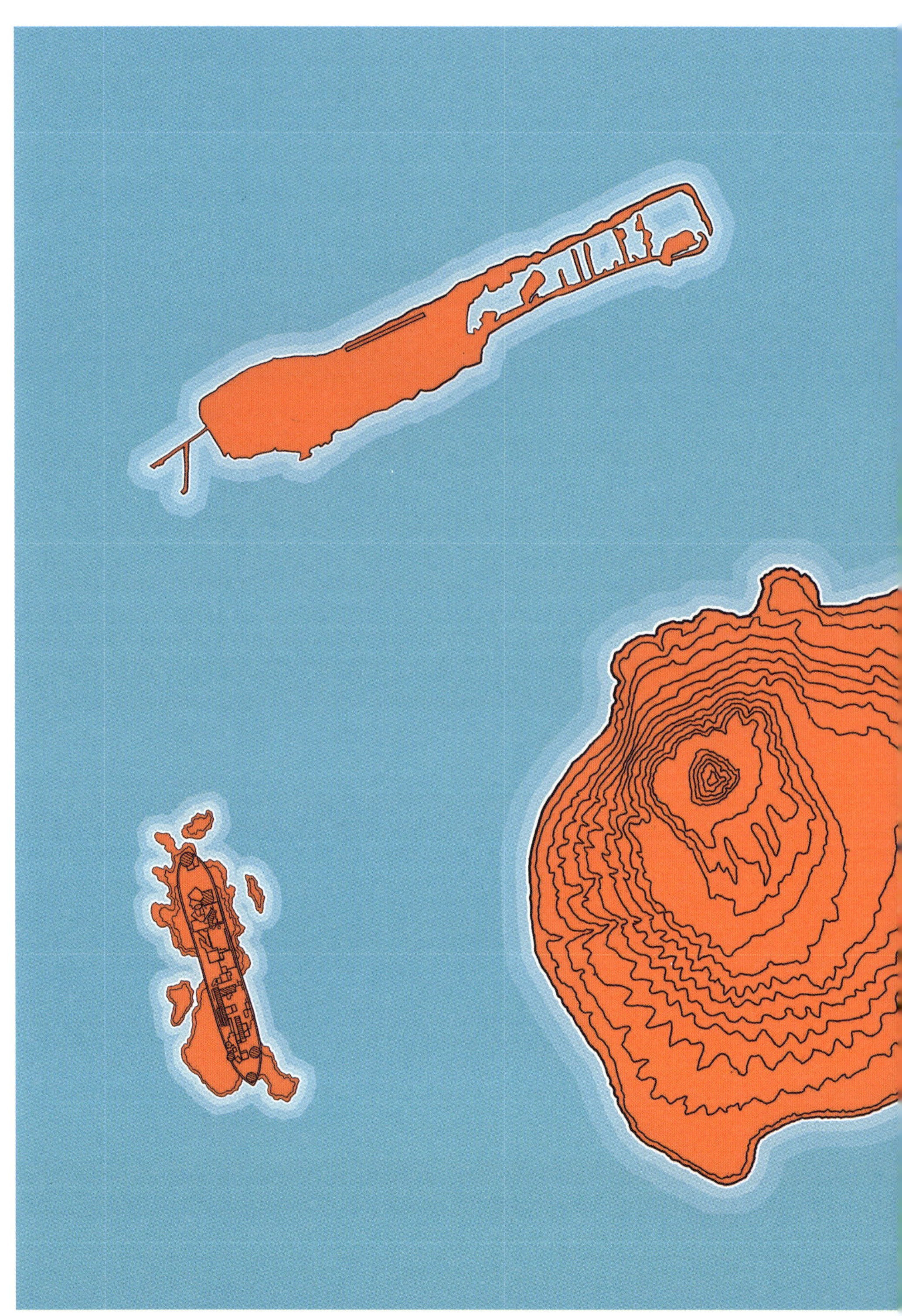

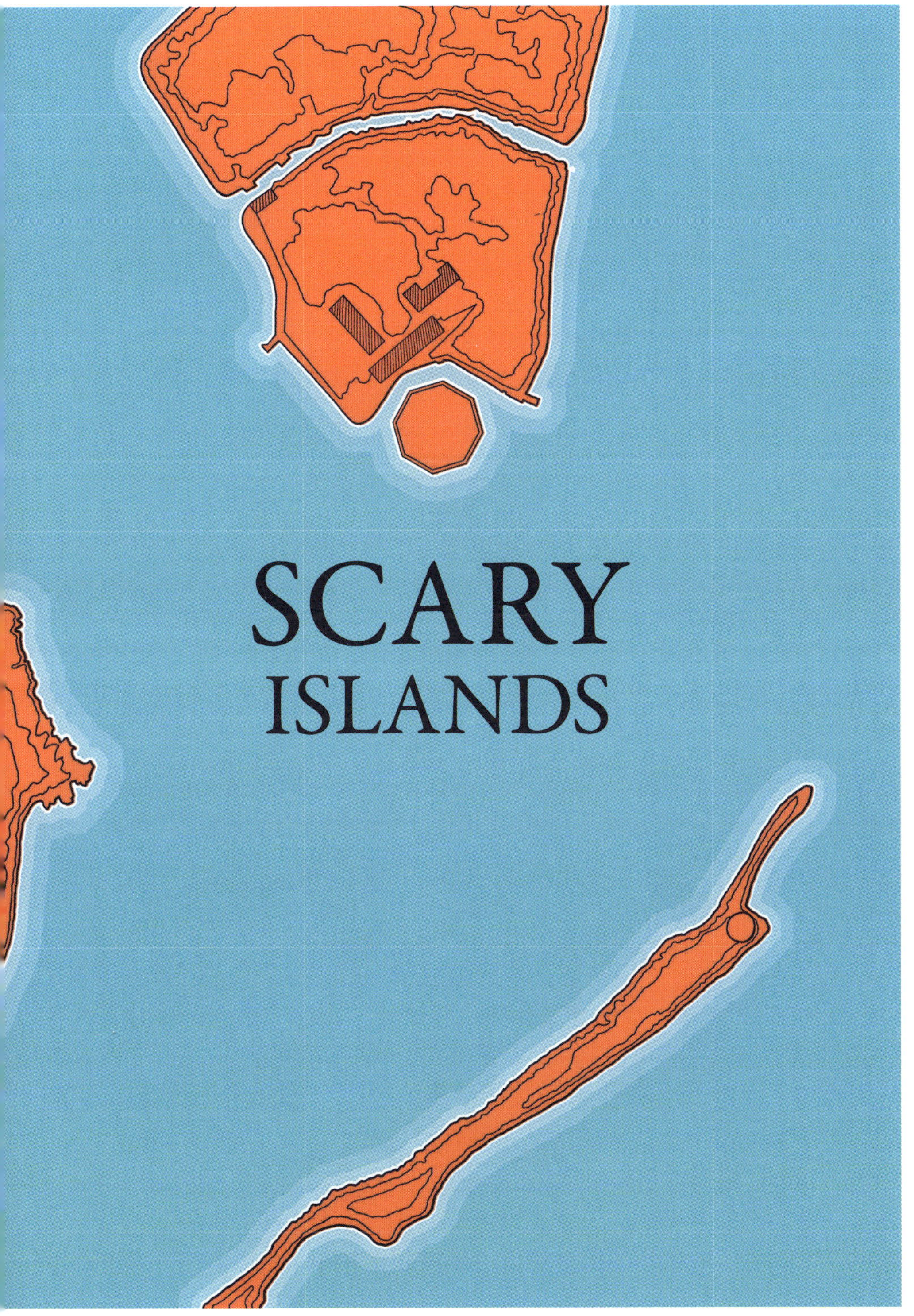

SCARY ISLANDS

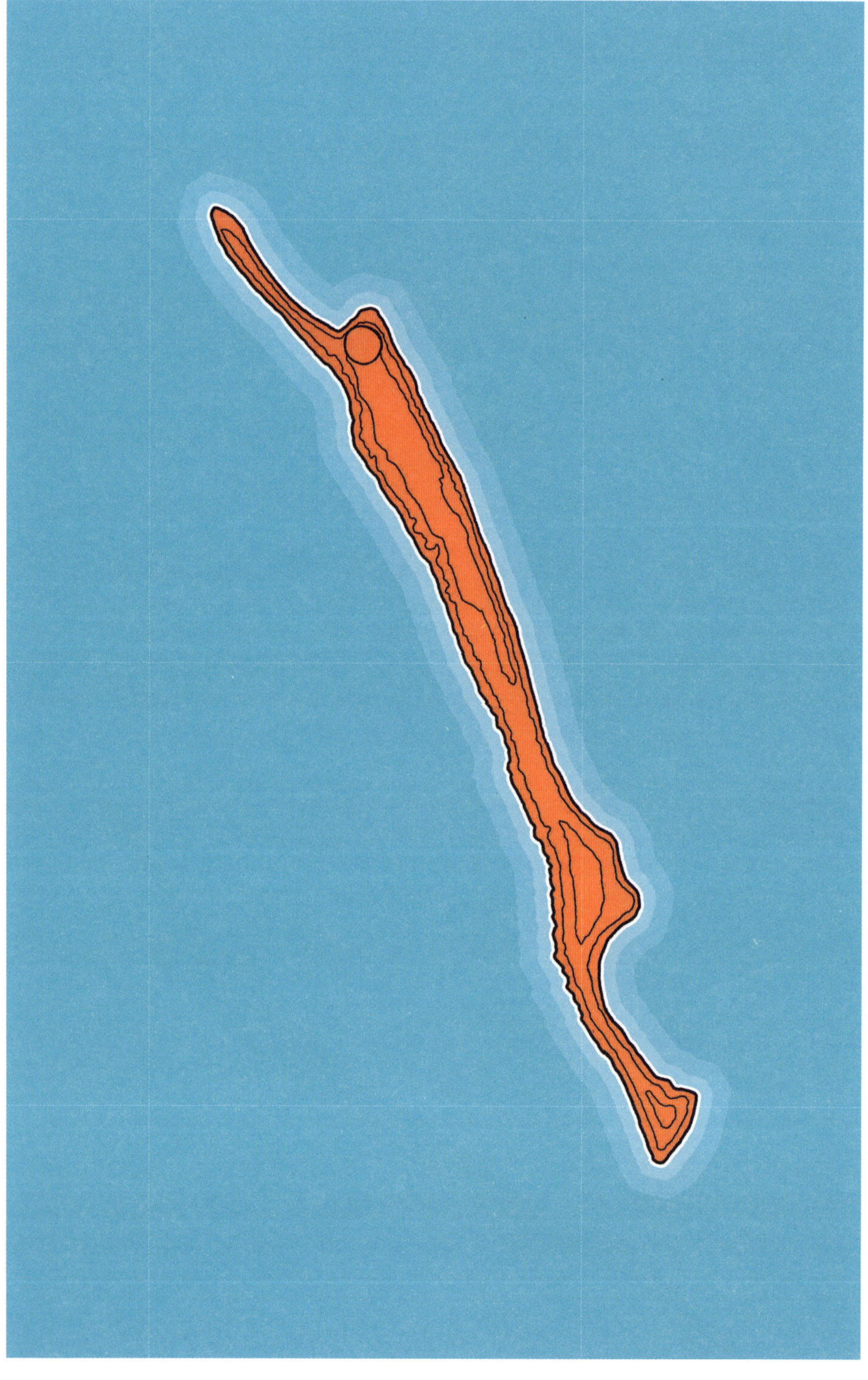

RUNIT
Monster Island

COUNTRY Marshall Islands **AREA** Approximately 317,700m² (3,419,694ft²). **POPULATION** Zero. **CHARACTERISTICS** An uninhabitable low-lying Pacific coral island and home of 'the Tomb' – a nuclear waste silo. Part of the Enewetok archipelago, which has a long history of occupation and destruction.

THIS TINY ISLAND is inhabited by a monster. A circular concrete dome squats malevolently at one end, packed with nuclear waste. There are no people here: this long, thin island is dangerous ground. Amid the tropical trees and on the margins of the hot white sands, the only living residents you might glimpse are nervous ground birds and dinner-plate-sized land crabs, shovelling their way past fallen coconuts.

The story of the island of Runit, with its 114-metre- (375-feet-) wide sarcophagus, which locals call 'the Tomb', transports us back in time to between 1946 and 1958 when the USA conducted forty-three nuclear tests on or close to Runit, and a further twenty-four across other islands in the Marshall Islands, most famously at Bikini Atoll. Many of these explosions were colossal: devices were donated with an impact hundreds of times larger than those that obliterated Hiroshima and Nagasaki.

The loop of thirty-four coral islands that contains Runit is called Enewetak, and it has the unwanted distinction of being the most nuclear-bombed place on Earth. Yet its story is little known and many would rather forget it. Who now wants to hear the name of Runit, or its near neighbour, the island of Elugelab, where the world's first full-scale thermonuclear test was carried out? On 1 November 1952, a bomb was donated on Elugelab with a force 700 times greater than the device that fell on Hiroshima. The island was vaporized. All that remained was a circular crater filled with seawater.

President Eisenhower was informed of the success of the test with the words, 'The island of Elugelab is missing!'. Other islands went the same way. A thermonuclear bomb was dropped on Runit in the same year. It exploded 450 metres (about 1,500 feet) above the ground, ripping away every living thing. Many more nuclear bombs were to follow yet, unlike some of its peers, Runit survived.

These blasts are among the biggest ever inflicted on the Earth. So, it is worth pausing to say that these islands were not empty but had been inhabited for 3,000 years. The environmental historian Todd Hanson tells us that they once resembled our clichés of paradise. Enewetak enclosed an 'azure lagoon, flourishing coral reefs and almost 200 kilometres [125 miles] of white sand beaches' he writes, it was 'an idyllic islandscape that was more than a hundred million years in the making'. This is what the first Europeans to encounter Enewetak would have seen. The very first was the Spanish explorer Álvaro de Saavedra Cerón, who came this way in 1529 and called this serene green necklace of islands 'Los Jardines' (The Gardens).

From Spain to Germany to Japan to the US, being passed between the hands of foreigners has been the fate of the Marshallese. In the twentieth century these transactions were to have dreadful consequences. During the Second World War Japan invaded Enewetak and in turn the Americans attacked in February 1944. A five-day battle raged, and thousands of soldiers were killed. In the end American firepower prevailed and, once victory was theirs, the Americans wasted little time in militarizing the islands even further. Soon it was a major US Naval Advance Base.

Throughout this time the islanders, the Enewetakese, clung on; spectators of wars in which they had no part, but which inflicted extraordinary violence on their homeland. Things were to get a lot worse. On 21 December 1947, the United States Navy relocated every Enewetakese to a distant atoll. Soon, the only voices to be heard in and around Runit were American. At one time 10,000 American scientists and supporting troops lived on Enewetak. The highest population ever seen on these islands was dedicated to one goal, to detonate bombs on them. Not just nuclear bombs: in the 1960s Enewetak was the primary target location for the testing of intercontinental ballistic missiles.

A story from a 1977 copy of *The New York Times* of a visit to Runit gives a unique window and primly describes a US nuclear safety officer escorting a gaggle of curious journalists on a visit. After a strict safety tutorial including a warning not to touch anything, the visitors are taken to 'two huge, deep craters filled with water' at the northern tip of the island. These craters 'had been gouged out of the coral and limestone by nuclear blasts' and it is explained that one of them will soon be put to use as the Runit Containment Dome (aka 'the Tomb'). The second remains a radioactive lagoon. In 1977 Runit was still littered with debris: pipes, buildings and a tower, a 'stark skeleton out of the past', once used to photograph mushroom clouds. The newspaper piece concludes that 'Runit must never be inhabited or cultivated' but mentions that while Runit is 'off-limits', seventy-five Enewetakese have recently returned to neighbouring islands 'to try to take up life where they left it thirty years ago'.

Over the past few decades, several hundred have come back. Most live a couple of islands down from Runit, less than 20 kilometres (12½ miles) away, where they have built an elementary school and make a living farming breadfruit, pandanus and coconuts. It is one of the world's most remote communities. The Marshall Islands, a scatter of island loops much like Enewetak, are a long way from anywhere: thousands of kilometres distant from Asia and Australia. From the capital, Majuro (a town that has 27,000 of the country's 42,000 inhabitants), you have to cross another thousand kilometres of ocean to reach Runit. These vast distances help explain why the Marshallese became expert mariners. For hundreds, probably thousands, of years, the islanders deployed so-called 'stick maps', exquisite three-dimensional objects using palm ribs and leaves to show the position not just of islands but also the flow and strength of ocean currents. Such was the intimate connection between the islanders and the sea that children would be blindfolded and set adrift, gradually learning how to identify their destination by the pulse and motion of the waves on the sides of their boats.

In many countries, the era of nuclear tests has receded into history, yet the Marshallese are still living with the consequences. The clean-up effort in Enewetak took decades to begin. Runit was the island chosen to be sacrificed: the Tomb was built in 1979 as a repository for contaminated material scooped up across all the Enewetak islands, including radioactive topsoil: it was all thrown in a pit and covered with concrete. But nuclear contamination has many afterlives. Serious health issues among the military personnel who participated in the clean-up have now come to light. And the Tomb itself is collapsing. The half-life of plutonium is measured in thousands of years. Not so concrete, which, when faced with stormy, salty seas, starts to crumble. Rising sea levels make this even more likely. A 2013 US Department of Energy report on Runit is a litany of alarming descriptions of deformations, cracks and leaks in the concrete shell.

Contaminated islands are best avoided: the water should not be drunk, seafood should not be eaten and plants cannot be farmed. Aside from the USA, other countries ravaged islands for the same purpose. The Soviet Union used Novaya Zemlya Island in Siberia; for the United Kingdom it was the Monte Bello Islands, off the coast of northwestern Australia; while France bombed the islands of Moruroa and Fangataufa in French Polynesia. About half of the world's twenty-six nuclear weapons testing sites were on islands. These places were chosen because they were far from anywhere, so the danger was deemed minimal. While it is true that they were remote from the nations that were bombing them, they were and are not seen as remote by countries in the Pacific where the tests and their aftermath remain an open wound.

At the height of its testing programme the USA was, on average, detonating one nuclear bomb a week. There are still thousands of such weapons, primed and ready to go, and they are distributed across an ever-wider pool of nations. However, with the exception of a test by North Korea in 2017, at time of writing not a single one has been tested since 1998. Photographs of mushroom clouds are familiar to us, but they have the reassuring patina of age. Test ban treaties can be credited but, in fact, the need for live tests was superseded by computer simulations. We are still living in the nuclear age; distant citizens of a tiny uninhabited island called Runit.

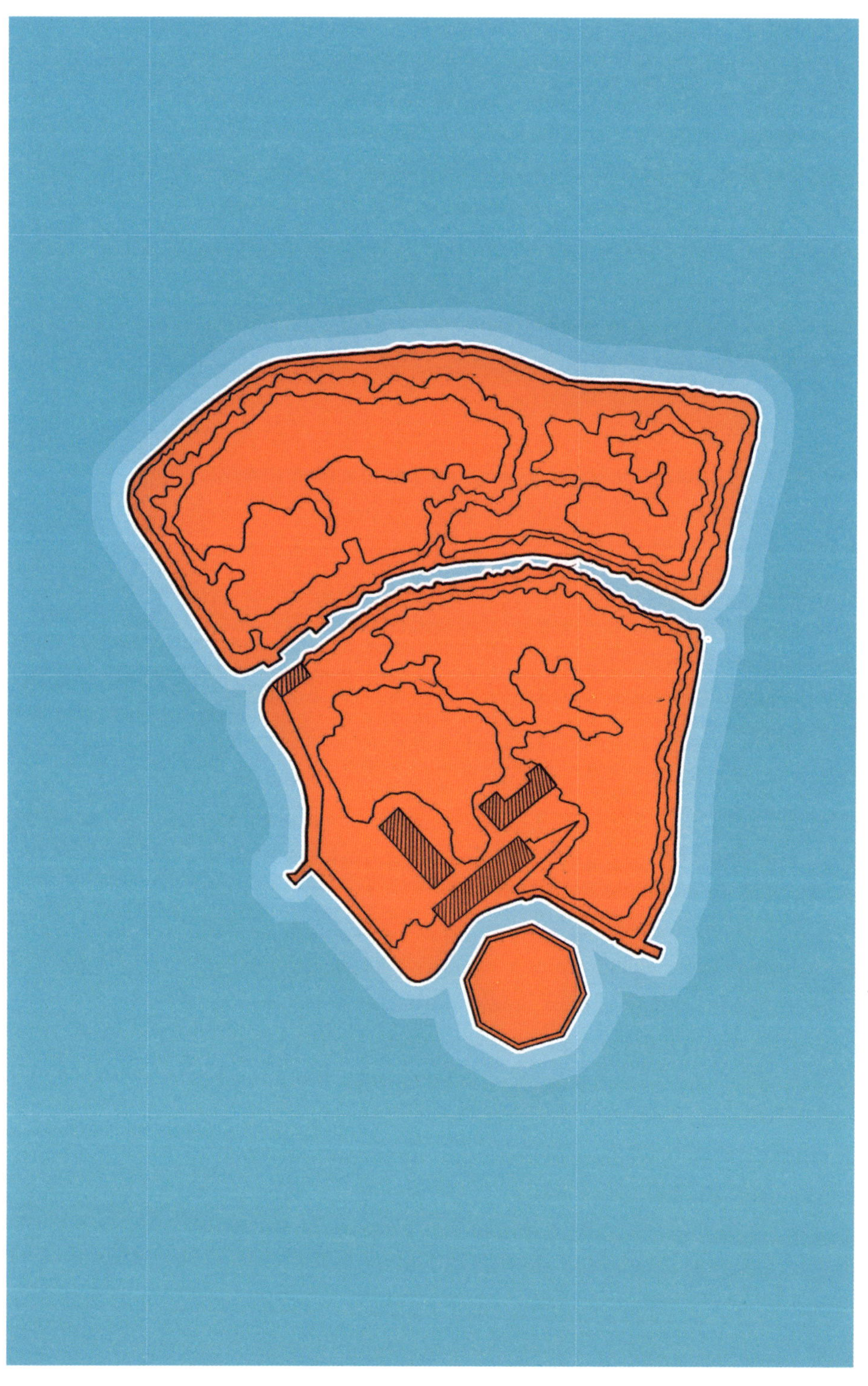

POVEGLIA

The Horror and the Lies

COUNTRY Italy **AREA** Approximately 82,000m^2 (882,640ft^2). **POPULATION** Zero.
CHARACTERISTICS An uninhabited island in the Venetian Lagoon. Over recent years it has become internationally notorious for its terrifying, spooky history. However, locals have a different story to tell.

ISLANDS CONCENTRATE EMOTIONS and ideas, both good ones and bad. In 1516 Sir Thomas Moore set his account of a perfect society on an island (he called it *Utopia*). In 1896 in *The Island of Dr Moreau*, H. G. Wells tapped into the equally powerful image of islands as places of captivity and terror.

Poveglia is said to be a real-life island of horror, a prison house of madness where half the ground is made up of human remains. Yet this is a legend with a twist in its tale. As we shall see, which story you believe about this Venetian island depends upon who you choose to listen to.

Despite visits being officially prohibited, Poveglia has become a coveted destination for 'dark tourists' in search of morbid thrills. TV and internet channels that specialize in spookiness have fixed their permanently wide eye on Poveglia. They repeat the claim that fifty per cent of the island's soil is made of human remains and usually throw in the local saying that 'a wicked man who dies wakes up in Poveglia'. It is regularly called the most haunted place in the world.

Let's a take a closer look. Poveglia is a wedge-shaped island, bisected by two short canals. Its population is zero and it is only 381 metres (1,250 feet) from its tip to its broad base. At its apex there is a striking artificial island, the eight-sided fort of Ottagono Poveglia; constructed around 1380 it was one of the first lagoon forts built to protect Venice. A little hop to the main island brings us to a dilapidated yet still elegant collection of old, empty, waterfront buildings, all institutional-looking and of mixed ages, with a church bell tower looming above. Scaffolding has been erected on part of the site, a sign of recent hopes for its redevelopment. For the time being, progress has ground to a halt and the weeds are threatening to take over.

Small islands have often been used to confine people and institutions not wanted on the mainland such as prisons, insane asylums, plague and leper colonies, but also weapons research facilities, airports and rubbish dumps. Poveglia's special character, its creepiness, appears to come from the way it combines a number of the least pleasant of these reasons and mixes them up into fertile soil for speculation.

Poveglia has been inhabited since the fifth century, but the origins of its legend start in the late eighteenth century when it was used as a quarantine station. *National Geographic* and many other sources attest that the island contains one or more plague pits with 'over 100,000' plague victims. A square stone block was placed on the cemetery, which is still there and bears the chiselled words: '*Ne fodias. Vita functi contagio requiescunt. MDCCXCIII*': 'Do not dig. Here lies contagion. 1793'.

In 1922 a hospital took over the island. Closed in 1968, it has been the wellspring of gruesome stories. The many films and online sources tell us that the hospital was an insane asylum and detail depravities, such as crazy doctors removing organs willy-nilly and conducting 'experiments' on live subjects. One of the doctors is said to have gone especially mad and to have begun torturing and killing the patients before they rebelled and tossed him to his death from the bell tower.

The American television series 'Ghost Adventures' filmed an episode on Poveglia (2009), while 'Scariest Places on Earth' (2001) devoted two episodes to it. The more films and blogs there are, the more ghostly stuff seems to happen on Poveglia, and the more dark tourists try to make it ashore. YouTube stories of Poveglia's spookiness multiply like mushrooms. Here, for example, is Matt Nadin, a salesman from Sheffield, who felt drawn to the island, because it's 'so full of dark, dark history, a hell of a lot of people died there. You really get a sense of the horrors that took place there while you're walking around,' he says, explaining 'they burned all the bodies and left them where they lay', then 'they started experimenting on them, horrible, horrible stuff'.

The chasm between these accounts and Venetians' own take on the island is vast. Indulging tourist fantasies has provided daily bread for Venetians for hundreds of years. Recently though, there is a new mood in the air. Some locals now think 'touristification' has gone too far and they want their city and its history back. Poveglia does have a dark history but it's not the cliché that has been spun for it. The 'local saying' that 'a wicked man who dies wakes up in Poveglia' is pure invention. Historian Alberto Toso Fei, who has written the definitive guide to Venetian ghost stories, says that it's 'sad to see how the island is being distorted'. He tells us that 'inventions spread across the web become "real" legends, but I would really like them to bring me even just one historical document that attests to their sources'.

The so-called horror hospital was a hospital with a psychiatric unit and a geriatric nursing home which, as one Venetian news site explains, was no 'different from what happened in other facilities throughout Italy'. A history website dedicated to documenting the city's very real and often lurid criminal history finds plenty of ghastly acts on the mainland, but nothing on Poveglia: 'No newspaper article reports doctors who committed suicide or cases of death on the island'.

Italy is a land of apparitions and superstitions, and the rationalist body called the Italian Committee for the Control of Claims on Pseudoscience (CICAP) has it hands full. Venetian members such as Riccardo Bottazzo find the idea that Poveglia is an island of terror rather hilarious. In the 'collective imagination' of Venetians, he explains, the island is 'the most peaceful place in the world. We all landed there as kids, in search of Stevenson-style adventures, aboard our first "cofano" [a small motorboat], the lagoon equivalent of a moped'. This rationalist debunker recalls that 'Poveglia was an obligatory stop to grill sea bass with friends', adding that there is 'no trace of ghostly presences on quiet Poveglia in all the rich literature on Venetian history and popular traditions'. In the Venetian history of Poveglia the island is more famous for its giraffe than its ghosts. In 1828, the Viceroy of Egypt sent a giraffe as a gift to Francis I of Austria, who ruled Venice, and the giraffe became a local celebrity, with Venetians flocking to the island to take a look.

What about the plague pits and the ground being made up of fifty per cent human bodies? Let's return to historian Alberto Toso Fei.

He tells us that only 'on two occasions did two ships of plague victims' get quarantined there. 'The first time in 1793 when 8 sailors died and the second in 1799 when 12 people died'; moreover, Alberto adds, 'We also know their names and surnames'. It is likely that some people died of disease on Poveglia at the start of the nineteenth century but if you want to find mass graves in Venice, there are much better places to look. The Venetians invented the idea of quarantine (the word comes from the Italian for forty days). Poveglia was just one of its quarantine stations, also called Lazzarettos. The oldest, Lazzaretto Vecchio, has plenty of mass graves. But it's not an island, and it lacks drama, so the media pass it by.

The idea that Poveglia is an island of horror is not going to be dispelled by rationalists and local fact-checkers but by a force far more powerful than either them or the unquiet dead: money. Local newspaper *Venezia Today* announced in 2024 that the island is 'up for auction: new hotels coming soon'. Such claims have been heard before but this time, we are promised, it's happening: the local municipality wants to sell the island on a ninety-nine year lease and the 'most haunted place in the world', will, perhaps one day soon, be echoing not with the groans of ghosts and the shrieks of dark tourists, but the mellow laughter and ice cube clinks occasioned by aperitivos on the terrace.

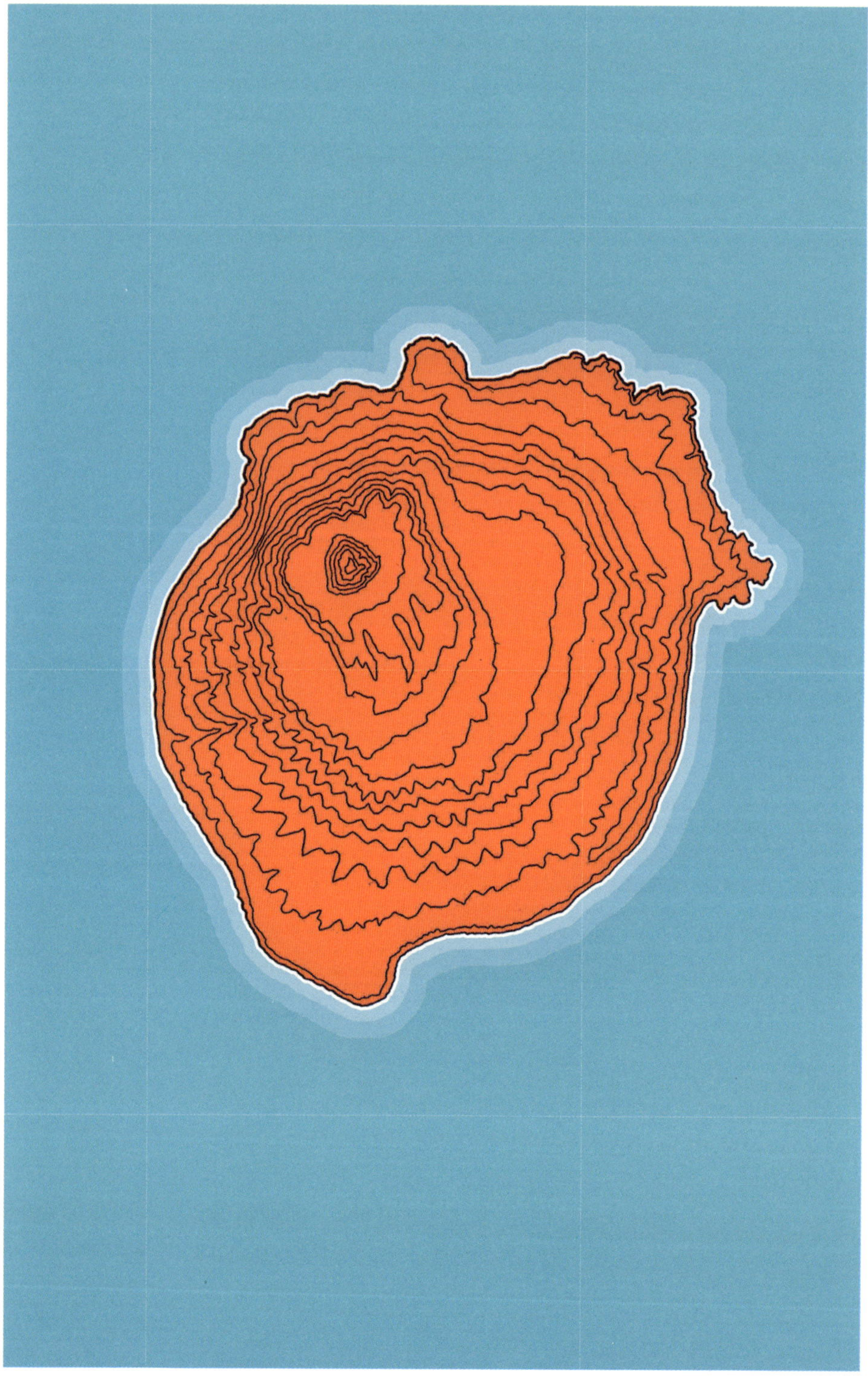

ANAK KRAKATAU

Child of Krakatau

COUNTRY Indonesia **AREA** Changeable; 2025 estimate: 2.85km^2 (1.1 square miles). **POPULATION** Zero. **CHARACTERISTICS** Grew in the caldera formed by the eruption of Krakatau; a very active volcano and dangerous neighbour to the millions of people who live on Java and Sumatra.

THE ERUPTION OF KRAKATAU in 1883 killed at least 36,000 people. Most died not from the explosion itself – which had a force 13,000 times larger than the atom bomb that destroyed Hiroshima – but the resulting tsunami. Two-thirds of the island was blasted into the air, leaving a residual mountain and a new sweep of sea. Fifty years later a new volcanic island, the 'Child of Krakatau' or *Anak Krakatau* in Indonesian, was born in the middle of this sea. The child is showing signs of being as dangerous as the parent. It is lively, unruly and often threatening. On 22 December 2018, hundreds of people died, and thousands were injured when Anak Krakatau erupted, causing its southwestern flank to collapse and triggering another large tsunami.

Before the 2018 eruption forests covered Anak Krakatau. The new explosion reduced the island to cinder and severed its peak to less than half the 338 metres (1,109 feet) it had gained since rising from the water. But the 'Child' appears to be in no mood to lie low. November 2023 saw plumes of volcanic material shooting 1,000 metres (3,280 feet) above its vent and a warning to the public to stay at least 5 kilometres (3 miles) from the crater. One resident of Sebesi Island 17 kilometres (10 miles) away, told reporters, 'We, the people of Sebesi Island Village, could not sleep since last night because the rumbling sound was loud like the sound of thunder'.

Volcanic eruptions are not deadly to humans because of their golden lava, their black, suffocating dust or the tsunamis that often accompany them. They are deadly because people get in the way. This is why, even though eruptions are not getting any bigger, they are becoming much more frightening. Over the past century the world's population has grown to such an extent that far more of us live in the shadow of a seething volcano.

Anak Krakatau does not loom over a city: it's a small island circled by three other small islands, namely Krakatau Island, which is what is left of old Krakatau, and Krakatau Kecil Island to the east and Sertung Island to the west. This is the Krakatau archipelago and today it is a nature park and uninhabited though there is a lively tourist trade catering to day-trippers who want to get as close as possible to the famous volcano. No one lives on Anak Krakatau but it is not as remote as it sounds. If you head east 60 kilometres (37 miles) you land on the island of Java, which has a population of 152 million. The first place you'll arrive is an industrial boom town, the steel city of Cilegon (population 450,000). Urban sprawl connects Cilegon to Serang City (population 700,000). Java is a busy, industrious and crowded island. Just 120 kilometres (74 miles) from Anak Krakatau takes you to the outskirts of its biggest city, Jakarta, the sprawling capital of Indonesia and home to 12 million people. The city's margins keep growing in all directions and include large areas classified as of high or medium risk from volcanoes. If Anak Krakatau were the only volcano to worry about the situation would be challenging but there are active volcanoes in many directions, especially to the southwest of Jakarta, near another big city, Bandung (where the population is 2.3 million).

Indonesia will soon have 300 million people, and it has 130 active volcanoes, more than any other country. Nearly all of them can be found along a line that runs through the islands of Sumatra and Java before curling up into Indonesia's scattered archipelagos. The Indonesian government has grand plans to move its capital from Jakarta to the island of Borneo, safely distant from this line of fire. This ambitious project is usually explained by reference to the fact that Jakarta is overcrowded, is sinking and faces severe flooding. However, its proximity to dangerous volcanoes is another part of the calculation.

Currently the big move is stalled. It's no easy task to build a new city and, even if the Indonesian government's main buildings do eventually get reconstructed in Borneo, it's quite possible that most of the population of Jakarta will be left behind.

We need to stop thinking of Anak Krakatau as a distant wonder and get used to the idea that it is a suburban volcano. Anyone looking at a map of Indonesia can see how huge cities and huge volcanoes rub shoulders. Humans have been living next to volcanoes for as long as there have been humans. The rarity and irregularity of eruptions meant that, for most of that time, nothing much happened. For example in 1916, Johann Handl moved to the relic island of Krakatau to mine its pumice. He leased one flank of the island for his business, where he built houses for himself, and his European and Indonesian workers. He lived like this for four years and walked away unscathed.

You and I would most likely be just as lucky. But it's dumb luck. Building cities near active volcanoes is dumber still.

All active volcanoes near population centres pose a threat but there are reasons to think that Anak Krakatau is more dangerous than most. There are localized geological forces at work here, rotating and pulling the rocks between Java and Sumatra and creating empty spaces for magma to fill. This means that magma rises easily here, something that can be seen by the speed of Anak Krakatau's growth. After it crested the waves in 1929, it grew at about 4 metres (13 feet) per year. The speed of Anak Krakatau's growth means that everything else also speeds up, including the likelihood of eruptions and rock collapses.

There have been lots of scientific studies of the 'Child' so its dangers are well known. A paper published by Thomas Giachetti and colleagues in 2012 foretold the nature and scale of the 2018 disaster and even calculated the height of the tsunami. Yet, in another sign that the danger of volcanism is more about human behaviour than geological drama, their predictions went largely unnoticed. It didn't help that, like most scientific studies, they were published behind a paywall.

Anak Krakatau poses a real threat to a lot of people. Like so many others I've traipsed around Pompeii and wondered why its 20,000 or so inhabitants were seemingly oblivious to the vast, smoking mountain that dominates the skyline. They had good reason to be oblivious.

They knew next to nothing about how volcanoes work. What is our excuse? Today not thousands but millions of people live in comparable settings.

The most profound lesson of the 1883 eruption was that our planet is not stable but shifting and its great geological forces are beyond our control. In *Krakatoa: The Day the World Exploded*, Simon Winchester argues that it shook old assumptions: 'Mankind, it seemed, was now suddenly really rather – dare one say it? – insignificant'. Since 1883 this message has been repeated many times. But it has still not sunk in. Today, as in the past, we base many of our most important decisions – such as where to build our homes – on the fond hope that we'll be lucky.

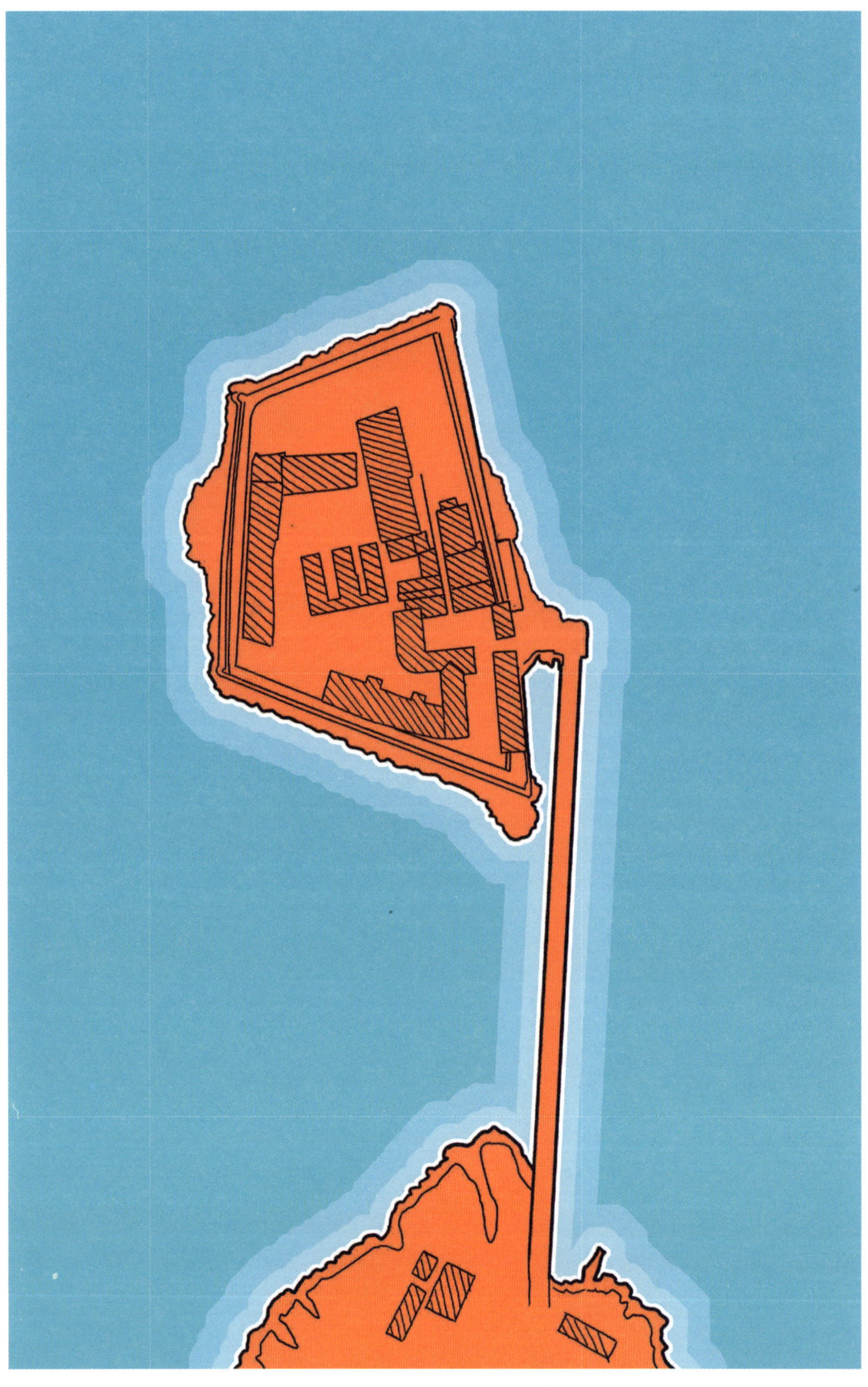

FIRE ISLAND

Russia's Prison Island

COUNTRY Russia **AREA** 19,700m² (212,049ft²). **POPULATION** An estimated 193 prisoners. **CHARACTERISTICS** A small island in a remote lake, housing a forbidding prison holding some of Russia's most dangerous murderers, but it has some surprising stories to tell.

IT'S EASY TO FORGET how horrible islands can be. They're pretty, they lure us in but what if you could never leave? Small islands are natural prisons: easy to monitor and hard to escape from.

Ognenny Ostrov, 'Fire Island', is a high-security facility housing nearly 200 murderers. It's a very small rhomboid-shaped island 380 kilometres (around 235 miles) east of Saint Petersburg in a lake that is surrounded by immense forests. The sides of the island are high walls, painted white, that plunge straight into the water, which is frozen for much of the year. There is a long, narrow and rickety plank bridge connecting Fire Island to a bigger island, Ostrov Sladkii, or 'Sweet Island', where the prison officers and their families live.

Fire Island is called 'Russia's Alcatraz' but it has a much longer history. It began life as a monastery about 500 years ago, when a local saint saw a pillar of fire on one of the lake's islands. Taking this to be a holy sign, he sailed across and, beneath an old spruce tree, built two monastic cells, one for himself, the other for future brethren. Other accounts tell us that Fire Island is the creation of zealous followers of a fourteenth-century holy man, Sergius of Radonezh. They were journeying through these wild lands when they saw tongues of fire leaping from a lake. In this version of the story, it was these men who built the island by filling boats with rock and earth and taking them to the spot where they saw the holy fire. They built a monastery and gave the island its name.

Beyond the myths there is one certainty: the conversion of the monastic cells to prison cells happened in the wake of the

Russian Revolution, when anti-Bolsheviks were imprisoned on the island. Fire Island then became one of many camps for victims of Stalin's purges. After Stalin's death and the end of mass political imprisonment, it was converted into a high-security facility for violent offenders, becoming dedicated to the incarceration of lifers (a moratorium was placed on the death penalty in Russia in 1996).

The prison is officially called Correctional Colony Number Five; only the island it occupies is called Fire Island, but Fire Island is the name that sticks. It is home to a depressing collection of serial killers, including racist killer Artyom Anoufriev, self-proclaimed cannibal Alexander Bychkov, and the so-called Apartment Maniac, Andrei Golovachyov. It's a brutal place for brutal people and perfect fayre for sensationalist click-bait. Among all the junk journalism that such places attract it is hard to find first-hand testimony of real people. One interesting account comes from a documentary filmmaker called Irina Vasilyeva. Vasilyeva became obsessed with a strange tale. It was about a love affair: a married woman, with three children, who, in Vasilyeva's words, 'falls in love with a prisoner – and a "lifer", at that – sentenced to life in prison for a particularly brutal murder. And for him, she abandons everything: her husband, her kids, her home'. Vasilyeva's film about this romance is called *Suffering* (Fishka-film, 2003) and culminates with a marriage service, officiated inside Fire Island.

Vasilyeva paints a vivid picture of the road journey to Fire Island:

> *Out the window everything seemed endless: the fields, the forest, the sky ... We kept going and going ... Finally, we turned off the main highway onto a country road ... And villages on either side – gnarled, slanting huts with broken fences, dogs and chickens wandering the streets.*

These endless tracks give Vasilyeva plenty of time to ponder Russians' complex and very gendered relationship with ideas of redemption and sin:

Russia has loved its prisoners since the dawn of the ages – they're sinners, but they're martyrs, too. They need comfort and consolation. There's a whole culture of pity, and its traditions are carefully preserved, especially in the small towns and villages. ... There are women who marry these habitual offenders, even murderers ... They're lonely. Suddenly, somebody needs them, they have someone to take care of. It's one way to change your life. A kind of medicine.

Vasilyeva talks to the bride, who holds little back, and is happy to tell her the desperate nature of her first visit to her beloved. 'She threw herself on the warden' and refused to go away. Her will to seek redemption, not for herself, but for another, appears noble, extreme and appalling.

On the door of each cell at Fire Island tradition dictates that a sign is hung detailing the brutal crimes committed by the inmate. Vasilyeva again:

You read them and are seized with horror, but then you go into the cell and meet a more-or-less normal person. He asks for a cigarette, you give it to him. 'What's it like out there? In here, we don't even know what the weather is.' They live on a rock. Surrounded by nothing but forests and swamps. No one has ever tried to escape ...

Today the island prison is a relic and Fire Island is probably on borrowed time. Islands have been used to exile and imprison for millennia, and in the distant past such islands were the most secure place to lodge someone you didn't want around. Today one of the few rivals to Fire Island is New York's Rikers Island and islands for asylum seekers, the largest of which is Bhasan Char, nicknamed 'Prison Island', a Bangladeshi island that is home to tens of thousands of Rohingya refugees. Prison islands have become obsolete. Modern technology provides unprecedented levels of lockdown, monitoring and surveillance. Nevertheless, these islands are lodged in our collective memory: an encapsulation of evil and isolation but also endurance and persecution. This is why they often have prosperous afterlives as tourist hot spots. Robben Island, around 7.5 kilometres (4.5 miles) from Cape Town is one of the city's most popular attractions. Alcatraz, in the middle of San Francisco Bay, once home to Al Capone, now swarms with day-trippers. The Îles du Salut, which include Devil's Island, was once a penal colony off the coast of French Guiana, immortalized by the 1969 memoire of Henri Charrière, *Papillon*. It too has found a new life as tourist attraction. It appears to be the inevitable fate of this genre of scary island: they are irresistible.

One day Fire Island will be welcoming day-trippers, its history mined for talismanic characters and grisly details. It won't be the only one. Another Russian prison island has been preserved as an icon of patriotic identity. In the far north on the island of Mudyug is the site of a concentration camp set up in 1918. The key detail is that it was built by the British and French. Outside Russia, people are often ignorant of the fact that thousands of soldiers from Britain and France, as well as the USA, Canada and Australia, invaded the country to attempt to scupper the Revolution. They were on the side of the White Russians in the Russian Civil War and soon after they docked at Arkhangelsk, they began imprisoning anyone who they suspected of being hostile to their mission. Jump forward a hundred years and the prison island of Mudyug has found a new purpose. A memorial complex has been established centred around the prisoners' bleak wooden huts. This tourist attraction is not troubled by crowds – it's a long way from anywhere, but its preservation has high-level political support. Here the threat of Western invasion can be kept alive and frozen in time. Fire Island holds one set of stories and Mudyug another.

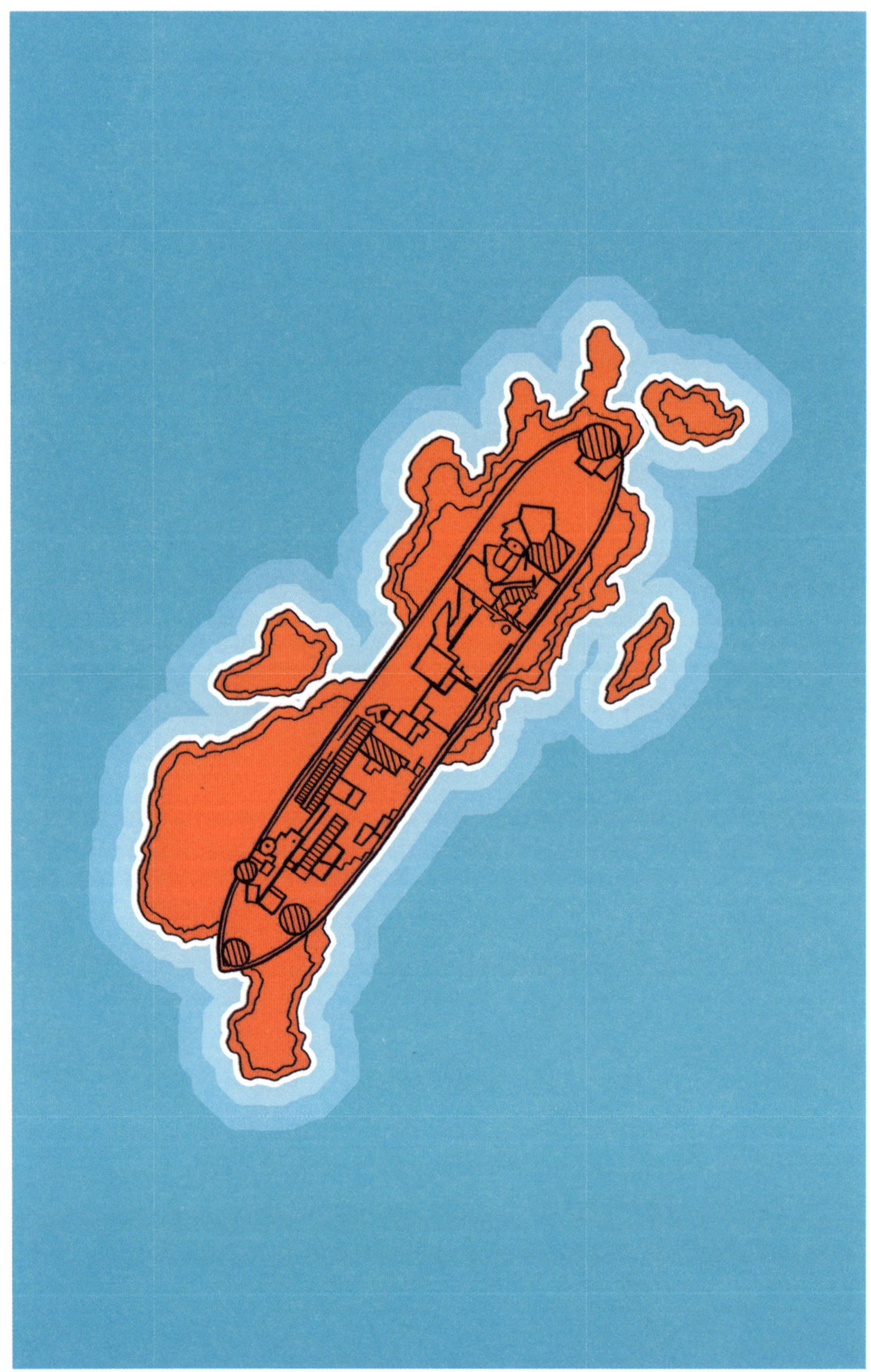

BRP SIERRA MADRE

A Frontline Island

COUNTRY Philippines **AREA** 1,230m² (13,240ft²). **POPULATION** Approximately 11. **CHARACTERISTICS** A dilapidated Filipino boat beached on the northern rim of a coral reef in a desperate ploy to peg back China's ambition to control the South China Sea.

THE BRP SIERRA MADRE is a dangerous billet. This broken ship, beached on a desolate reef, is the Philippine's rusting frontline in a dispute with China about its territorial claim to almost all of the South China Sea.

It may be a wreck, crewed by eleven unlucky marines, but geopolitically it is a global hot spot. The ship is not seaworthy but remains in commission and offers a bold declaration that this is Philippine sovereign land. The Philippines, backed by the USA, does not want to cede the South China Sea to China. The Chinese Navy has fortified numerous similar reefs into naval harbours and planted them with airstrips big enough for long-range bombers. The Chinese Coast Guard regularly harasses Philippine ships. The ruling of the Permanent Court of Arbitration – an international body that tries to settle intergovernmental disputes – that there is 'no legal basis for China to claim historic rights' over the islands of the South China Sea, counts for little in Beijing.

At any time, this standoff could turn into a war. The future is uncertain and the past has been a litany of trouble. In the 2020s the *Sierra Madre* sits high and, depending on the tides and the weather, sometimes dry, on the northern rim of a looping reef called the Second Thomas Shoal. It's a little less than 200 kilometres (125 miles) from the Filipino island province of Palawan, and well within the Philippines' exclusive territorial waters, which extend 200 nautical miles (370 kilometres) from its shore. But so too is Mischief Reef, which has been seized and fortified by China. Today China has de-facto control over the South China Sea, penning in the Philippines, as well as Indonesia, Malaysia and Vietnam (though see Barque Canada Reef entry, page 91) to an uncertain coastal strip.

The BRP *Sierra Madre* (the BRP stands for 'Barko ng Republika ng Pilipinas'– 'Ship of the Republic of the Philippines') could easily be overrun by Chinese forces. In 1998, seeing what was happening to other islands in the area, the Philippine president, Joseph Estrada declared he wanted to 'put up our own structures' and the 100-metre (330-foot) long *Sierra Madre*, along with a sister ship, were run aground on the reef. The Chinese saw this as a provocation and Manila tried to appease its concerns. The second ship was removed. But the *Sierra Madre* remained, and in 2014 was declared to be a 'permanent installation'.

A BBC report about life aboard the *Sierra Madre* paints a sorry picture: 'The ship's sides are peppered with massive holes. Waves slosh through them right into the ship's hold.' There is little to do, and there is a lack of food and basic provisions. The Chinese Navy does not block every supply ship but enough to make things perilous and uncomfortable. A game of cat-and-mouse has been set in motion, with the Filipinos using fishing boats to dodge the blockades and weaving through shallow waters where the big Chinese ships cannot follow.

Aware that the *Sierra Madre* is in a terrible state the Philippine Navy began patching it up. In 2023, improvements to the ship's sleeping quarters and galley were made, and an internet connection established, making life on board this maritime relic a little more bearable. But having got wind of this upgrade, the Chinese Coast Guard fired a green laser at supply vessels, which the Filipinos said caused temporary blindness among the crew. Rear Admiral Roy Vincent Trinidad, of the Philippine Navy, remains defiant: 'BRP *Sierra Madre* will remain, we will not give up that ship'.

The *Sierra Madre* is already a survivor: it has had many lives and seen many battles. Its long career began in 1944, as 'USS *LST-821*'. 'LST' stands for 'landing ship, tank'. It was built in Indiana, for the

57

amphibious transport of tanks and other vehicles. *LST-821* spent its war in the Pacific, supplying American island bases. After the Second World War *LST-821* was renamed the USS *Harnett County* and entered the Vietnam War. It was refitted to accommodate 266 men and became a base for the Mekong Delta Mobile Afloat Force. In 1970 it was transferred to the South Vietnamese Navy and became RVNS *My Tho*. When Saigon fell to communist forces *My Tho* became an escape ship, its deck and cabins filled with 3,000 refugees on a one-way passage out of Vietnam. But the fleeing *My Tho* had to pass through Philippine waters and the Philippine government recognized communist Vietnam, not its defeated southern adversary. Some clever negotiations by the US Ambassador to the Philippines, William Sullivan, smoothed its passage and allowed for a temporary reflagging. It became, once again, a US ship, and was allowed into the Philippines, where its desperate passengers disembarked at Subic Bay. It was here, after lying in dock till 1976, that its final name and flag were agreed: BRP *Sierra Madre*, a ship of the Philippine Navy.

How can the Chinese government justify trying to seize islands within its neighbours' territorial zones? It is high-handed but relies on China's long-standing claim to all the islands of the South China Sea, from any of which it could then claim the 200-nautical mile (370-kilometre) exclusive economic zone. In a statement to the United Nations the Chinese government explained:

> *China has indisputable sovereignty over the islands in the South China Sea and the adjacent waters, and enjoys sovereign rights and jurisdiction over the relevant waters as well as the seabed and subsoil thereof... The above position is consistently held by the Chinese Government and is widely known by the international community.*

Taiwan makes the same assertion, on its own behalf. Although 'waters' are spoken of, it is the islands that really interest these two governments. Ships sailing through don't much concern them but the occupation of 'their' islands, even uninhabitable reefs, does. The idea that all these rocks are Chinese has become a tenet of national geography, one found in Chinese schoolbooks. One secondary school geography book explains 'The southernmost point of our country's territory is Zengmu Ansha [James Shoal]', which is a reef currently held by Malaysia and a mere 83 kilometres (52 miles) off its coast. The editor of *Chinese National Geography*, a monthly magazine similar to *National Geographic*, tells us that the idea that the South China Sea is Chinese is 'now deeply engraved in the hearts and minds of the Chinese people'.

Since these islands are uninhabited – or at least they were before recent military colonization – and a really long way from the Chinese mainland, the fervent nature of the Chinese claim on them may seem curious. It cannot be separated from the rise of China to superpower status nor from how Beijing sees that the USA gained control over huge areas of the Pacific by dint of its island possessions (Hawaii, American Samoa, Guam, Northern Mariana Island, as well as several atolls. In addition, the Marshall Islands, Federated States of Micronesia and Palau cede a range of government functions, including defence, to the USA; see Runit, page 60). China's claims are modest by comparison.

What does China conclude? To hem in its ambitions? To be like the USA? Both and neither. China has a huge military but, in contrast not only to the USA, but also to Russia and some European and Gulf states that currently support one side or another in distant conflicts, it advocates non-intervention and prefers to stand back. From a Chinese perspective, China is both patient and restrained and Beijing finds it galling to be told that it cannot exercise control over its own backyard by countries that stomp across the world.

This is the Chinese perspective. For those Filipino marines, bored and anxious, wandering the decks of the *Sierra Madre*, a blockaded and beached ship that lies *within* their country's internationally accepted maritime territory, this wider context will sound both fantastical and beside the point. The Philippines is no threat to China, yet China is pushing its way on to its shores.

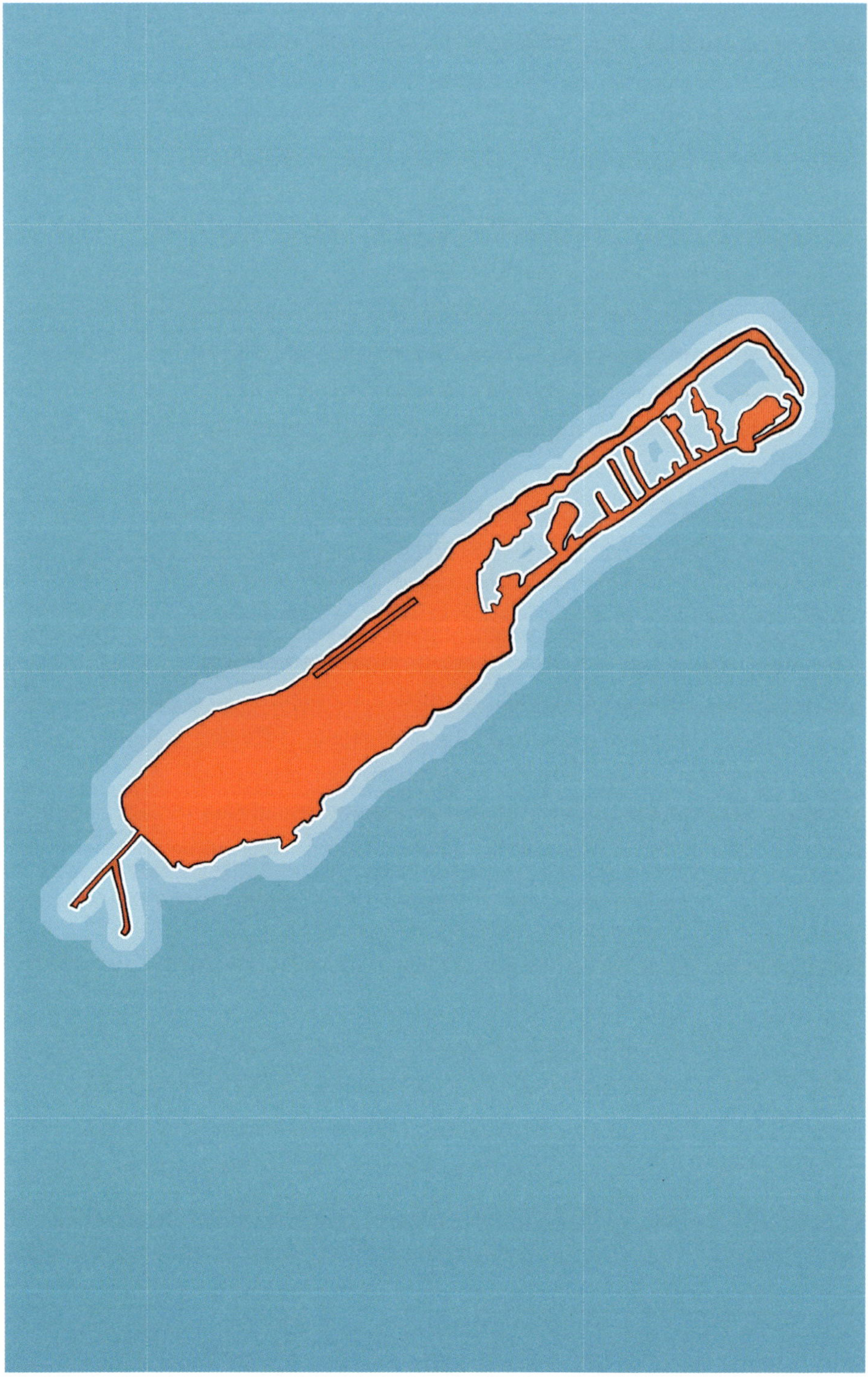

BARQUE CANADA REEF

Vietnam's New Military Islands

COUNTRY Vietnam **AREA** 1.66km^2 (0.64 square miles). **POPULATION** Unknown. **CHARACTERISTICS** A coral reef; one of the Spratly Islands occupied by Vietnam. It joins a growing collection of platforms, islets and reefs that Vietnam has been turning into military outposts.

CHINA RULES THE ROOST in the South China Sea. It has built substantial military islands and by doing so it has grabbed control over most of these waters. But not all. For China is not the only country that is concreting over coral reefs and turning them into landing strips and garrisoned outposts. Barque Canada Reef, one of the Spratly Islands, is a natural reef 27 kilometres (17 miles) long and up to 5 kilometres (3 miles) wide. Vietnam has had a military presence on the island since 1978 but recently it has turbo-charged its island-building activities and Barque Canada Reef has been pumped up and bulked out, making it one of the largest of the many weaponized islands in this hottest of geopolitical hot spots.

The South China Sea is well acquainted with outlandish island-making schemes (see Ocean Flower on page 46, and BRP *Sierra Madre* on page 84). Once home to tranquil blue lagoons, alive with delicate corals and a long way from the cares of the world, it is now a building site. The waters around Barque Canada Reef are called the Dangerous Ground because of the profusion of ship-ripping reefs but today's dangers are far from natural.

Barque Canada Reef is a thin tapered loop of beaches and islets 585 kilometres (363 miles) from the Vietnamese mainland but only 63 kilometres (39 miles) from Mariveles Reef, another militarized reef and one of five controlled by Malaysia. To the north lies Firey Cross Reef, the most radically transformed Chinese outpost: it has been reshaped into a harbour for gunboats of all sizes and has a runway long enough to land the largest of bombers. Further on is Taiping Island, a sawn-off, malformed and concreted-over ex-reef controlled by Taiwan. These are just a few examples: the whole area is a muddle of battle-ready mutant islands, and they are nearly all claimed by multiple countries. There is little logic to who controls what, other than who got there first.

China is the main player in these waters but it's not playing alone and at the start of the 2020s Vietnam began to rapidly expand its firepower. Its islands and platforms are now dotted across a sweeping arc of what the Vietnamese call the East Sea. The Washington-based Asia Maritime Transparency Initiative (AMTI) has been tracking all the islands built by Vietnam and its neighbours and tells us that, so far, Vietnam has reclaimed a total area of about 9.55 square kilometres (3.7 square miles), which is about half the area that China has reclaimed. AMTI's researchers have also found that Vietnam now occupies around fifty outposts spread across what they call 'twenty-seven features' in the South China Sea. This figure includes fourteen isolated platforms that resemble low-slung oil-rigs but also appear to be military installations. In terms of numbers of new islands, Vietnam is currently outpacing China.

Like a lot of the reefs in this area, the internationally recognized name of Barque Canada Reef refers to a nineteenth-century trading ship wrecked upon these shoals. It's a fitting name: the island is ship-shaped: its Vietnamese name is *Bãi Thuyền Chài*, or Fishing Boat Beach. A Vietnamese news site boasts that the island is 'an ideal geographical entity to build a strategic military airport and, at the same time, with the depth around the coral reef, the Vietnamese Navy, in the right conditions, can build and fill a large seaport as a dock for warships and a storm shelter for fishermen'.

The expansion is focused on the island's middle strip, which is being beefed up to accommodate a considerable runway and naval base. It has nothing like China's military capability but Vietnam seems to be trying to emulate China's new islands. Which begs the question: what is Vietnam doing? There is an island-building arms race in progress

but it's a very odd contest. It has been set in motion and, in large part, already won by one participant – China. Vietnam's aims are different. It does not claim ownership over the whole of the South China Sea, but it doesn't want to cede it either.

China keeps testing Vietnam's resolve. In 2014, it placed an oil drilling rig within Vietnam's 200-nautical mile (370-kilometre) exclusive economic zone. This provoked a standoff in which the Chinese turned water cannons on Vietnamese boats and anti-Chinese protests broke out across Vietnam. China has continued to probe Vietnamese reactions, regularly sailing its navy into its waters. 'We will resort to every means possible to make sure we can defend and safeguard our legitimate interests in the East Sea', a spokesperson for the Vietnam's Ministry of Foreign Affairs told *The Washington Post*.

Vietnam's island-building frenzy is basically defensive, yet it has developed a life of its own. The problem is that building islands is now easy. The scale of the modern boats that do the heavy lifting – which are called 'cutter sucker dredgers' – and the ease with which multiple pipelines can be used to pump sediment, means that in shallow seas, especially those with reefs, islands can now be roughed up in a matter of months. It is made even easier when there are few people speaking up for the marine environments that are obliterated. Multiple habitats across this once beautiful sea have been destroyed but those who do raise the issue are being ignored. I suspect future generations, especially but not only in South East Asia, will look back at what is being done here as a source of shame and a kind of madness.

At the time of writing Barque Canada Reef is still being built, although this is true of most of these islands: they are constantly being added to and expanded. They are never-ending projects. Since Barque Canada Reef's military base is located in the middle of the island, which is a long thin loop of beach and coral, it doesn't have to rely on floating cutter sucker dredgers but makes use of land-based diggers to extract sand from different parts of the island. Clamshell or grab dredgers can also be used, which reach out over the water to gouge out sediment. Everything dug away is then transferred on to trucks, which drive on Barque Canada Reef's only road, built for the purpose, across the short distance to its ever-growing airstrip. Researchers from AMTI have also spotted concrete and metal pillars for docks and piers around the island, as well as the construction of a coastal defence structure that could be used to house artillery.

'What Hanoi is signalling to China is this: "Don't push us too hard"', says Huong Le Thu, an Asia-focused analyst at the International Crisis Group. It's a balancing act: Vietnam wants good relations with China but also with the United States. The US has been providing it with security assistance and arms but Vietnam shares a 1,300 kilometre (800-mile) land border with China, which is also its largest trading partner. It makes no sense for Vietnam to try and 'take on' China too directly. Its island-building programme displays a stagey assertiveness and this seems to be the point: Vietnam wants China to see that it won't be humiliated and won't easily concede the 'East Sea'. It's building fast but, says Nguyen Hong Quan, a Vietnamese major general, it doesn't want to provoke. 'After all,' he says, 'it's China that started this.' He's right, but Vietnam's burst of island building has its own strange momentum, which is starting to look divorced from either practical or symbolic needs.

Military islands freckle the planet. There are hundreds of them and the more there are, the more governments claim to need. They are extraordinary things. But each is a potentially dangerous flash point. And each transforms a natural environment, a unique marine habitat that has been growing and evolving for thousands of years, into concrete and metal.

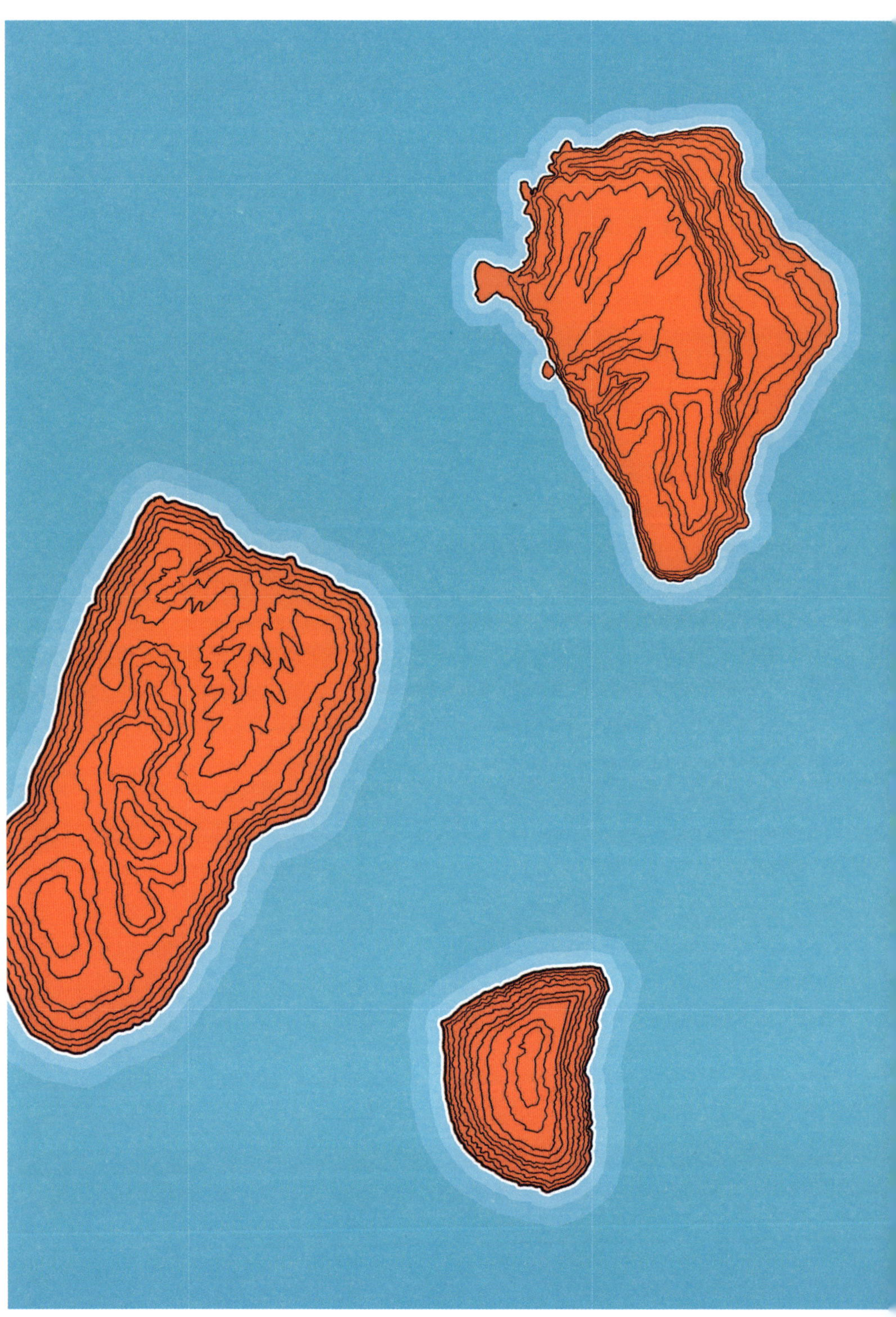

REMOTE ISLANDS

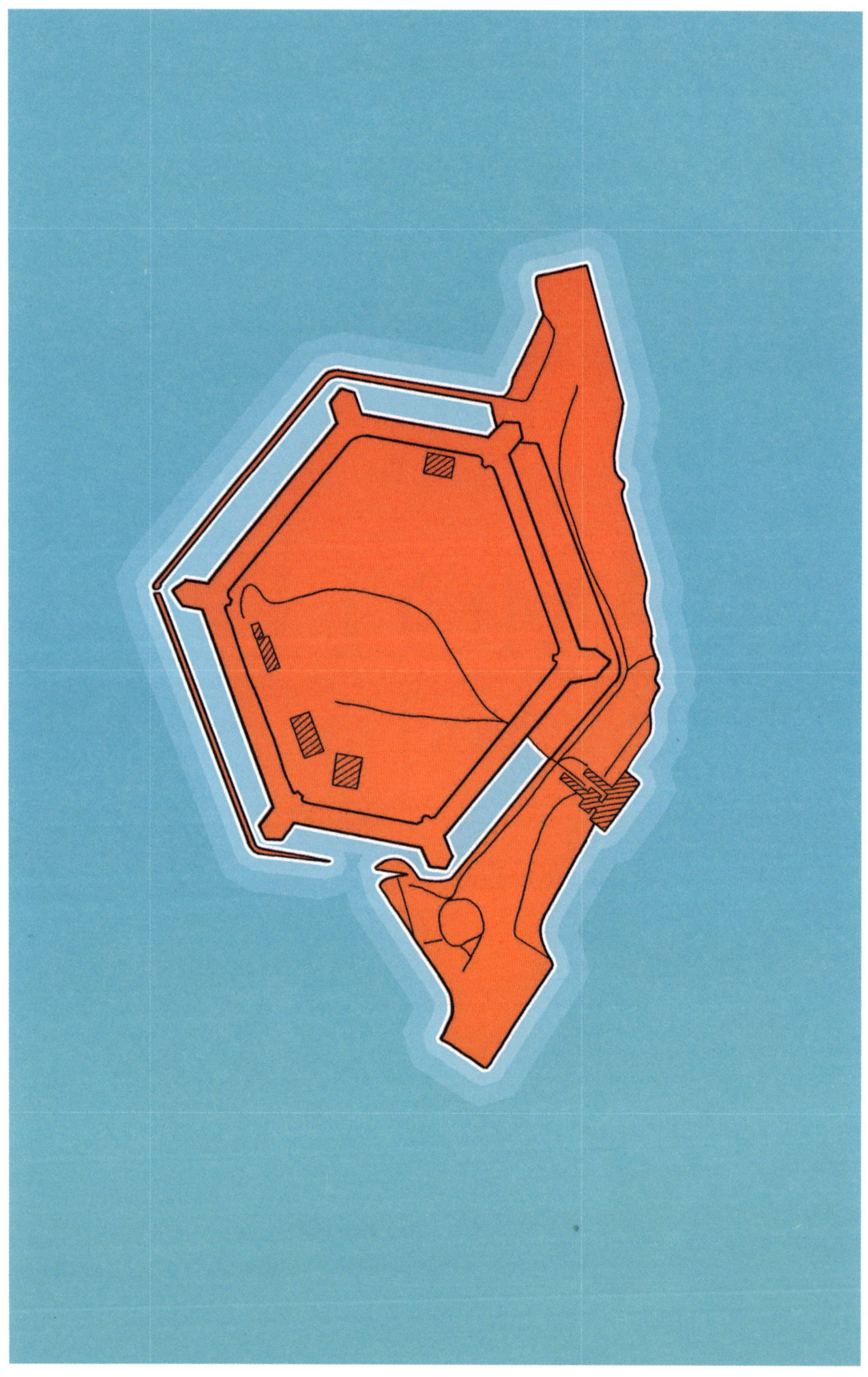

FORT JEFFERSON

America's Distant Fortress

COUNTRY United States of America **AREA** (Garden Key): Approximately 93,000m^2 (1,001,000ft^2). **POPULATION** Approximately 10 (National Park Service personnel). **CHARACTERISTICS** An enormous and forbidding brick fort sitting on a distant and tiny island in one of America's most remote national parks.

FLORIDA, THE MOST southerly state of the continental USA, has a curling tail of islands that whips out into the Gulf of Mexico. You can drive from Florida's southern tip over a series of bridges and thin islands and in a couple of hours you'll be in Key West. There you'll find museums dedicated to the town's luminaries, Ernest Hemingway and Tennessee Williams, but also a dock. There is a ferry waiting and it goes to one of the farthest edges of the USA.

A little over 100 kilometres (62 miles) beyond Key West, is one of the world's most incongruous sights: Fort Jefferson. The massive ramparts of the largest brick building in the Americas rise out of a shallow sea. It's a lumbering hexagon made of sixteen-million handmade bricks and it was built as a military and penal outpost between 1846 and 1875. Today it is a remote tourist attraction. Fort Jefferson is the star attraction of Dry Tortugas National Park, one of the more obscure and far-flung of the USA's National Parks. It has seven tiny islands or keys (Garden Key – which is largely covered by Fort Jefferson – as well as Loggerhead, Bush, Long, East, Hospital and Middle) but no fresh water, hence the name. Otherwise Dry Tortugas National Park is far from dry: it is ninety-nine per cent salt water.

There is a long history of islands being used as military forward placements, and across the world they continue to be the front line of defence and attack. The azure shoals around Fort Jefferson appear calm but Havana is only 170 kilometres (106 miles) away and every year the Dry Tortugas sees hundreds of refugees pitch up on its sandy shores. The drama is not all political: storms regularly barrel through these reefs and inundate the islands. In 2023 an underwater graveyard was discovered. One large headstone bore the name John Greer, and the date 'Nov. 5. 1861'. Who was he and what happened to him? It's a mystery. His life and his resting place now lie fathoms deep.

For most of its history the Dry Tortugas were uninhabited. The Spanish conquistador Juan Ponce de Leon bumped into them in 1513. He found plenty of turtles and so named the place the Tortugas (Spanish for turtles). The turtles were a source of meat for de Leon's hungry sailors and remained so for generations of sailors. The turtles are still there, thankfully no longer hunted. In the centuries following de Leon's visit, the Dry Tortugas were used as a pirate base. Many ships were raided from these islets and these seas still lure treasure hunters. The most famous recent find was the wreck of the *Nuestra Señora de Atocha*, a Spanish galleon. It was discovered in 1985 along with its golden haul, about $450 million worth of gold, silverware and emeralds.

Why the fort was built goes back to a forgotten war. The War of 1812 was fought between Britain and the USA. It lasted a year or so and its purpose continues to puzzle historians. However, one thing the war did achieve was a resolve to protect America's southern and eastern coasts. Fort Jefferson was to be the jewel in the crown of a series of maritime defences initially envisioned to stretch from Maine to Texas. Spain ceded Florida to the USA in 1819 but not a few naval officers thought the new fort was a silly idea. Commodore David Porter visited the islands in 1825 and wrote a damming report:

The islands consist of small sand Islands a little above the surface of the Ocean, on some of which is some low shrubbery, but all are liable to changes from gales of wind. Their insulate situation, and distance from the continent renders blockade easy ... they have no fresh water, and furnish scarcely enough land to place a fortification and it is doubtful if they have solidity enough to bear one.

It was not until 1846 that work began. In *America's Fortress*, historian Thomas Reid tells us that the 'challenge was similar to building on another planet: every brick, every plank, every stone and every worker shipped in from some distant point'. As many of the workers were convicts and enslaved people, they were not just building a military fort and a naval harbour but their own prison. It was, says Reid, a 'castle of vast walls and towers rising from the mists of a blue-green tropical sea, defying all logic and stereotype'. Such was the demand for bricks generated by Fort Jefferson that new factories and even new brick-making techniques were called for. A patent for automated brick production was filed in 1858 to meet its needs; it was an invention that promised to 'turn out 40,000 bricks per day', though lack of government funding stymied its further development.

Another Florida historian, Albert Manucy, paints a vivid picture: 'Slaves were the backbone of the labor gang, sweating in the broiling sun, sloshing in the tepid water, digging the foundations for the ponderous walls, dumping barrow after barrow of mortar into the forms'. The slave owners lived in Key West and were jittery about the possibility of escape. In his account Thomas Reid adds some telling details of just how jittery. In January 1860, he explains:

> *Key West's slave owners were thrown into panic by an entirley baseless rumor that the slaves at Garden Key had somehow all escaped to Nassau in the Bahamas ... and the atmophere was not improved by allegations that the slave who assisted the blacksmith had been forging spear points in his lesiure hours.*

Escape was more than a rumour. In 1847 seven men had taken off on a boat and disabled the schooners that would be sent to capture them. They sailed eastward and seemed to have gained safety. Unfortunately, their pursuers were just as persistent, and all seven men were recaptured and returned to Fort Jefferson and enslavement.

Slave labour on Fort Jefferson came to end in 1863. Convicts now became the sole source of forced labour. Many of them were military deserters but they also included men imprisoned for political dissent as well as rape, robbery and murder. Fort Jefferson became one of America's largest prisons. Remote, hot and bone dry, it came to be known as 'Devil's Island'. The most famous inmate was Dr Samuel Mudd, who was sentenced for giving medical help to John Wilkes Booth after he had assassinated President Lincoln. Mudd went from villain to hero when yellow fever swept the fort. He convinced prison officials to put in place a hygiene regime and his recommendations saved many lives, and earned Mudd a pardon and an early release.

Although Florida was on the Confederate side in the Civil War, Key West and Fort Jefferson were a Union stronghold, and were used to blockade the southern states. Passing ships may have been able to dodge Fort Jefferson's guns, but they were easy targets for the Union ships that sailed from its harbour. Fort Jefferson, built to ward off any attack, was a major asset for the Union side. It had 420 heavy-guns, with corner bastions allowing defensive fire across the walls. At its peak nearly 2,000 men lived at Fort Jefferson.

By the 1880s the military's interest in this remote fort was coming to end. It was too distant and too expensive to run, and in 1888 the Army turned it over to the Marine-Hospital Service to become a quarantine station. In the early twentieth century, it began its current life, as a tourist and wildlife sanctuary. In 1908 the islands were designated a bird reserve, then in 1935 a National Monument, before finally, in 1992, becoming a National Park. There is nowhere like it: Fort Jefferson erupts from the ocean, vast, lonely and incomparable.

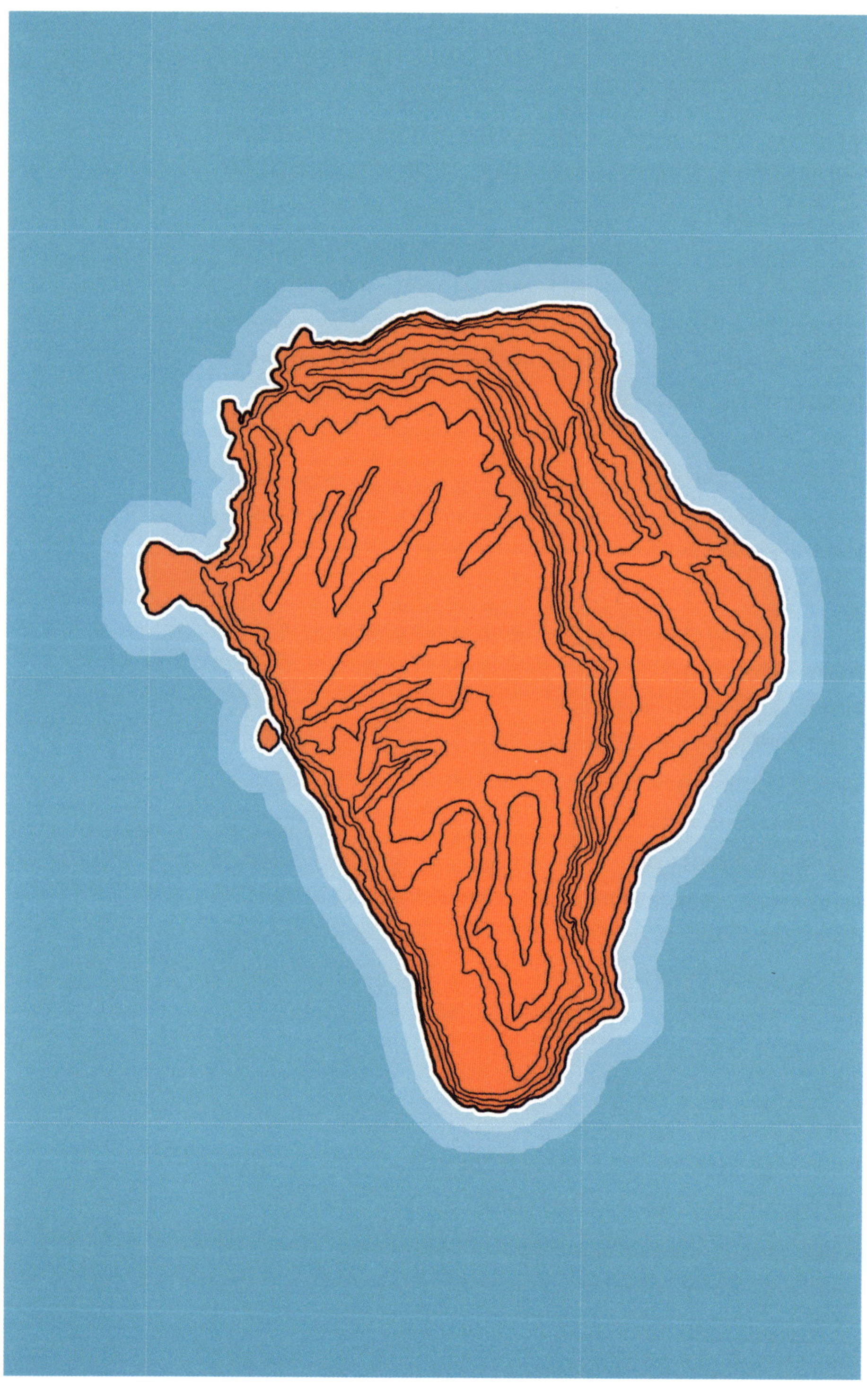

INACCESSIBLE ISLAND

The Farthest Shore

COUNTRY United Kingdom **AREA** 12.65km^2 (4.88 square miles). **POPULATION** Zero. **CHARACTERISTICS** A rarely visited island, it has been unforgiving to those who have tried and remains one of the world's least disturbed ecosystems.

IN A WORLD WHERE everywhere and everything appears instantly available Inaccessible Island is a stubborn holdout. Its huge vertical cliffs bolt up from uninterrupted ocean. There is one short strip of pebble beach where you can moor a small boat but some of the world's roughest storms and powerful currents mean it's only possible to land during a rare break in the weather, which typically occurs in December or January, and lasts a mere week or so. Few have come and few ever will.

Inaccessible Island is an uninhabited, rhomboid-shaped island, 5.7 kilometres (3½ miles) wide. It's in the middle of the South Atlantic, 31 kilometres (19 miles) southwest of Tristan da Cunha, which itself has a good claim on being the most remote inhabited place on Earth. Tristan da Cunha has a population of 238 but it has no landing strip. The only way of getting there is by sea: a seven-day voyage from Cape Town.

Inaccessible has no people but it is not true to say it is empty. It is a uniquely protected ecosystem: there are no rats, cats or land mammals of any kind. Nor are there any reptiles, amphibians, butterflies or snails. Yet it is a garden of wild things, green with all kinds of plants, buzzing with insects and the home of myriad birds and seals.

The Inaccessible Island rail, the world's smallest flightless ground bird, is found only here. The absence of invasive mammals means that this small brown bird is left in peace, the modest king of a small kingdom. Inaccessible rails are reclusive but on the island they are everywhere: pecking their way through the tall grasses and bushes or among the island's thirty-seven unique flowering plants and ferns, perhaps alongside the Inaccessible bunting, another species found nowhere else. On other islands both would have been extinct long ago: their eggs would have been eaten by rats. But Inaccessible, like its sister, Gough Island, are among the world's least disturbed natural habitats. Designating them as a World Heritage Site UNESCO described the two islands as 'one of the most pristine environments left on earth'.

Despite its dainty dimensions the Inaccessible rail has a mythic status among naturalists. HMS *Challenger*, the Victorian science ship that can be said to have invented the sciences of bathymetry and oceanography, made a detour just to find the famous 'Island hen'. The vessel's chief scientist, Sir Whyville Thomson, wrote that 'it is one of very few regrets that we found it impossible to get a specimen of it'. To help understand why, one of the island's few recent visitors, the conservation biologist Brian Gratwicke, describes it like this: 'It's like a giant wedding cake, with very very steep cliffs, just dropping off straight into the sea'. High above the steep crags that ring the island, lie broad grassy uplands, cut through with streams that pour off the cliffs in spectacular waterfalls. These upland regions are really hard to reach. On the island's strip of beach and single access point, where mooring buoys make landing possible, visitors are confronted with an expanse of steep, pathless ground that soon terminates in yet more vertiginous cliffs. So even if you do make it here, the beach is as far as you can go.

The fortress-like nature of the island means that its wildlife has no experience of humans. 'When we got to Inaccessible Island', Gratwicke continues, 'it was pretty amazing, because none of the birds had any fear of people,' they 'would walk right up to you and nibble on your fingers.'

The Tristan da Cunha archipelago was discovered and named after the Portuguese explorer Tristão da Cunha in 1506. It took another 150 years before Inaccessible was spotted. That came in 1656 during a voyage by the Dutch ship *Nachtglas* (*The Night Glass*) and, until its acquisition by the British, the island was named Nachtglas. In the

centuries following, it become an irregular stopover for the fishing, seal and whale hunting industries. Yet Inaccessible has never been a lucky island for humans. Several attempts were made to settle but they soon unravelled. Inaccessible is one of those difficult places where the conceits of human dominance, even of mighty empires, get washed away.

The only famous event the island is known for is the now-forgotten scandal of *The Blenden Hall*. At around 10 a.m., on 22 July 1832, a British ship, *The Blenden Hall*, bound for India and crowded with colonial families, ran aground on the island's outlying rocks. The ship was smashed to pieces but the whole of its forecastle broke loose and, along with all but two of the eighty-four passengers and crew, was carried safely on to Inaccessible's shore. However, rather than displaying the plucky, indomitable British spirit expected of children of the Empire, the survivors were quarrelsome, panicked and untrustworthy. For four months they survived on penguins, albatrosses, diverse eggs and seal meat. The published account by Alexander Greig, son of the ship's commander and one of the survivors, scandalized Victorian readers:

> *The passengers and sailors were sitting indiscriminately around; the latter, mad with liquor, were quarrelling and nearly murdering one another, and at length they commenced grossly insulting their more helpless shipmates, particularly the passengers; swearing, with the most horrid imprecations, that they would kill and eat the children when next in want of food. The screams and terror of the females were dreadful in the extreme.*

Greig tells us that 'during the confusion', the sailors 'contrived to rob the passengers of their cloth by piecemeal, till finally many who stood cowering round the flames had scarcely a rag to cover them'. The thefts and fights were to continue and attempts to build a boat and sail to Tristan ended in failure and the death of six people. It was a miserable and rag-tag party that was eventually rescued.

The next unlucky arrivals were German brothers Gustav and Frederick Stoltenhoff, who came ashore in 1871 hoping to make the island a trading base for seal skins. There is a photo of them from a couple of years later standing with the party of British sailors who rescued them. They stand in front of the hut they had cobbled together, made of what looks like branches and reeds. The South African author and distant relation of the brothers, Eric Rosenthal, told their pathetic story in *Shelter from the Spray*, published in 1952. It's a tale as much comic as tragic. We certainly feel for the two young would-be entrepreneurs: 'The gales howled almost incessantly across Inaccessible,' Rosenthal writes, 'and the waves, piled up for thousands of miles across the Atlantic, reached such mountainous heights that even on solid land the adventurers were appalled.' But it is Gustav and Frederick's ineptness that sticks in the mind. They forgot to bring any rope or candles and had no experience of slaughtering and skinning animals or of building a shelter, and what they did build was repeatedly blown to bits.

Inaccessible does not just push people away, it makes fools of them. Even the local Tristan islanders have given up on it. They used to make a few visits each year to collect eggs and to kill the sheep and cattle, goats and pigs that had been shipped over to the island. But Inaccessible was too far and too hard. Even the descendants of these animals have now perished. One final effort to establish a human presence was made in 1936 when a settlement of fourteen souls was established on its meagre beach land. The settlers tried to farm potatoes, but the crop failed and, within a couple of years, they too had thrown in the towel.

Today, other than the odd conservationist, no one comes to Inaccessible Island. In an overcrowded planet it's a place that provokes contradictory desires. Some see it as a challenge. Human fascination has a voracious quality: there will always be those who want to stick a flag on the farthest spot. Yet perhaps we can take comfort from the fact that Inaccessible is left in peace, protected by towering waves and high cliffs, and that the little Inaccessible rail can peck through the tall, untrodden grasses, curious, trusting and safe.

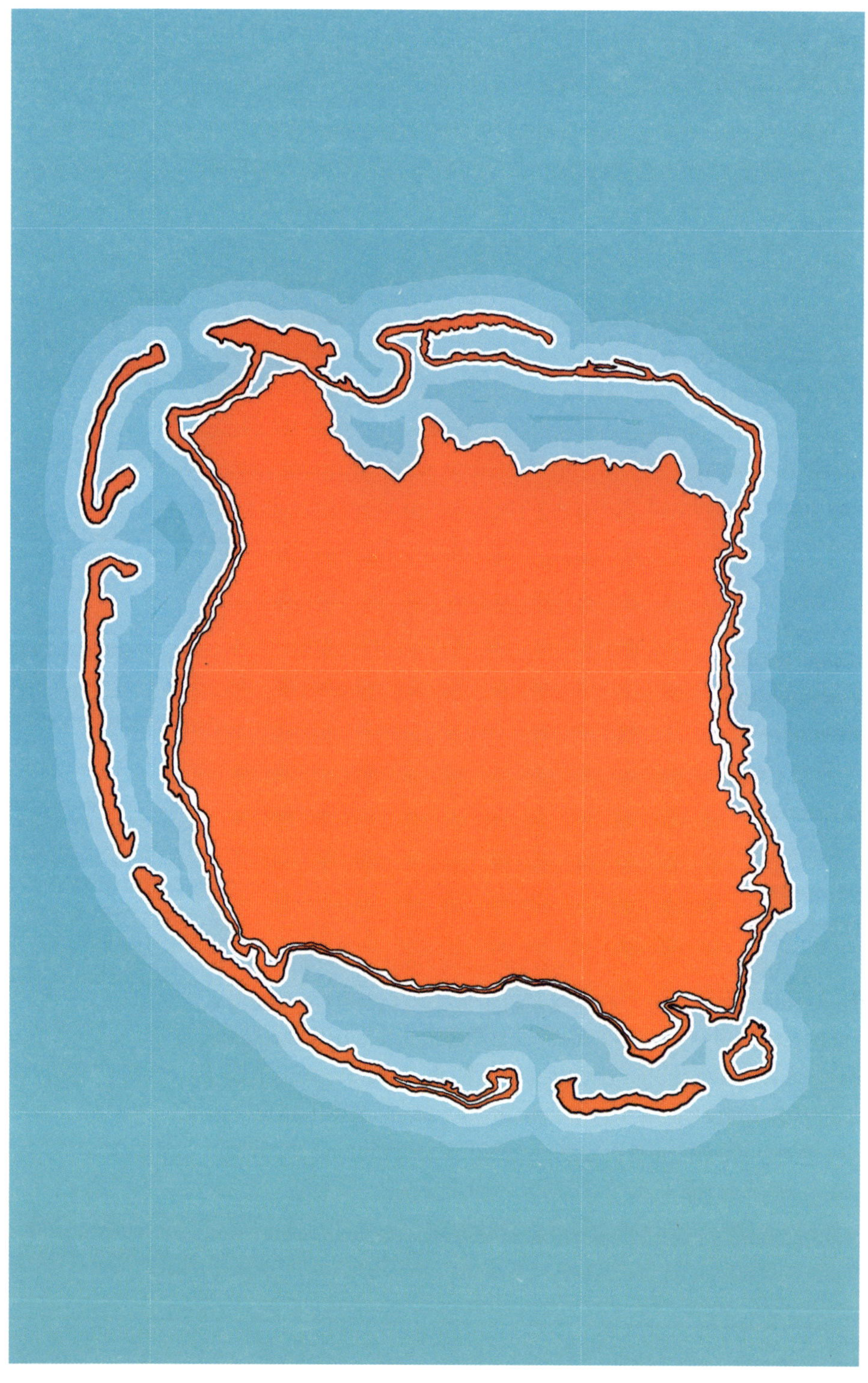

NORTH SENTINEL ISLAND

Modern Survivalists?

COUNTRY India **AREA** 59.67km^2 (23 square miles). **POPULATION** Unknown. Estimates range from 50 to 200. **CHARACTERISTICS** The legendary last and only 'uncontacted' island, the story of Sentinel changes when we understand it in the context of what has happened to other tribal groups in the Andamans.

ISLANDS ARE FIXED and usually small and they are often understood by way of fixed, small stories. For many decades the story about North Sentinel was this: it's 'the last island'; a unique remnant; the only island inhabited by an uncontacted and totally isolated people, a belligerent tribe from the Stone Age, adrift from the world.

It's an alluring idea. Despite North Sentinel being tiny and its population being, maybe, a couple of hundred, it has generated a steady stream of documentaries and books. Global public interest was boosted in 2018 when John Chau, a twenty-six-year-old American missionary, ignoring the prohibition on landing on the island enforced both by the Indian government and common sense, splashed up its sandy beach shouting 'My name is John. Jesus loves you'.

A Sentinelese boy responded by shooting an arrow through the Bible that John was brandishing. The normally smiling and enthusiastic young American beat a hasty retreat. Unfortunately, he didn't learn from his experience. That night John wrote two questions in his diary: 'Why did some little kid have to shoot me today. His high-pitched voice still lingers in my head' and 'Lord is this Satan's last stronghold?'. He returned, presumably with the same kind of greeting.

Soon after, fishermen spotted his corpse being dragged away and buried by Sentinelese. The Indian authorities tried to recover the body but after a standoff on the beach it was decided no further attempts would be made.

We don't know their language, customs or religion. But the Sentinelese are not a remnant of the Stone Age. They are survivalists. North Sentinel is the last redoubt of the indigenous people who once dominated the long archipelago of 200 islands that make up the Andamans, a union territory of India in the Indian Ocean that lies a few hundred kilometres away from Myanmar and a thousand kilometres away from Kolkata, the nearest Indian city. The diverse tribes who are collectively called the Andamanese have lived on these islands for 55,000 years, maybe more. Since the arrival of colonialists and settlers over the past couple of hundred years, they have been almost completely exterminated, in large part by measles and other diseases. Today they make up less than one per cent of the population of their homeland. North Sentinel is their last redoubt.

The person who understands North Sentinel best is the Indian anthropologist Triloknath Pandit. As a young man he tried to contact the Sentinelese several times. However, as he studied and thought more, Pandit began to think he had been wrong to try and become friends with them. He became a critic of intervention, of any kind, and guided India towards a policy of zero contact. Today he argues that contact, however benign its intentions, will have destructive consequences. The Sentinelese, he explains, 'see what has happened to other tribes' and are right to be wary. Pandit adds that 'outsiders coming there with friendship in their hearts can do a lot of damage'.

When Pandit speaks of 'what has happened to other tribes' he is not simply referring to their near total replacement by settlers from India, who today constitute almost all the Andaman's 435,000 population. What has 'happened to other tribes' is a reference to the fact that, while a few groups cling on, most no longer exist. The Jangil, who originally inhabited Rutland Island, were extinct by 1931; the last individual was sighted in 1907. The process of extinction is still underway. In 2010 a woman called Boa Sr died: she was eighty-five years old and the last speaker of Bo, one of ten original Great Andamanese languages, nearly

all of which are now dead. 'Since she was the only speaker', explained an Indian linguist who knew Boa Sr, 'she was very lonely as she had no one to converse with'.

Like the rest of India, the Andamans were once under British rule. The idea that the Andamanese were a primitive and doomed race guided colonial relations with them. One of the most chilling reflections of this approach was the behaviour of Maurice Vidal Portman, superintendent of the Andaman Island Penal Colony between 1879 and 1901. He breezily strolled on to North Sentinel and soon came across many tracks, a few abandoned villages and, after a few days, six Sentinelese, who he promptly kidnapped. He took them – two adults and four children – to the capital, Port Blair. His account of what happened next is unsentimental: the adults 'sickened rapidly, and the old man and his wife died'. The surviving four children were returned to North Sentinel. In Portman's book *A History of Our Relations with the Andamanese*, it is clear that, for him, whatever happens to what he calls these 'savages', is unimportant because of the 'rapidly approaching extinction of the race'.

The long history of contempt for the Andamanese may have started with the British but it continues today and, just as in the past, is mixed with fascination. In high season, roads through the archipelago's main hub, Great Andaman, can be jammed with tourist vehicles on a kind of human safari, hunting out elusive tribal people. The threat of disease has also not gone away. The 400 members of one of the few surviving groups on Great Andaman, the Jarawa, have only been in regular contact with the outside world since 1998, when a few Jarawa started to emerge from the forest to visit nearby towns. There then followed two outbreaks of measles, in 1999 and 2006, and other predations were to follow. With the opening of a main road through their territory, the Jarawa became a tourist commodity, valued as exhibits. There are also many reports of Jarawa women being sexually abused by poachers and other settlers.

We don't know for sure, but it seems likely that the Sentinelese know very well what the outside world has in store for them. Their island has been under assault for a long time. The idea that the Sentinelese are deliberately choosing to avoid the fate of kindred tribes is driven home by looking at a map. Just 40 kilometres (25 miles) of sea separate North Sentinel from Great Andaman, where hundreds of thousands live; a few kilometres more will take you to the capital, Port Blair. The basic outrigger canoes that appear to be the only craft available to the Sentinelese are punted rather than sailed and would not take them far from their island home. But this does not mean they have no knowledge of the outside world. Not only do they probably have memories and stories of past attacks, but all sorts of travellers have come their way, rarely in ways that ended well.

The fact that the Sentinelese don't care for strangers was driven home years before John Chau's 2018 visit, when they killed two fishermen whose boat had drifted on to their shores in 2006. Sunder Raj and Pandit Tiwari had anchored offshore but during the night their open-topped boat came adrift. The draft from the rotor blades of an Indian coastguard helicopter hovering over a North Sentinel beach revealed their bodies buried in shallow graves. Like John Chau, to date they remain on North Sentinel. Should the killing of Sunder Raj, Pandit Tiwari and John Chau go unpunished? It would be hard to argue any of them deserved their fate. They were murdered and murder is wrong. Yet it is also obvious that invading North Sentinel and hauling people before a court, would not be an act of justice. The Sentinelese are not asking for anything except to be left alone and they appear to know that 'contact' means extermination.

Advised by Triloknath Pandit, the Indian 'Master Plan' for the island is both clear and wise: 'the Sentinelese do not require the benevolence of the modern civilization', all they require is 'non-interference'. No visits, no toys, no coconuts, and no Bibles are allowed, only an occasional observation from what the 'Master Plan' calls a 'respectable distance, say 50 metres [165 feet] from the shore'. The survivalists of North Sentinel know enough about us to refuse our hand of friendship.

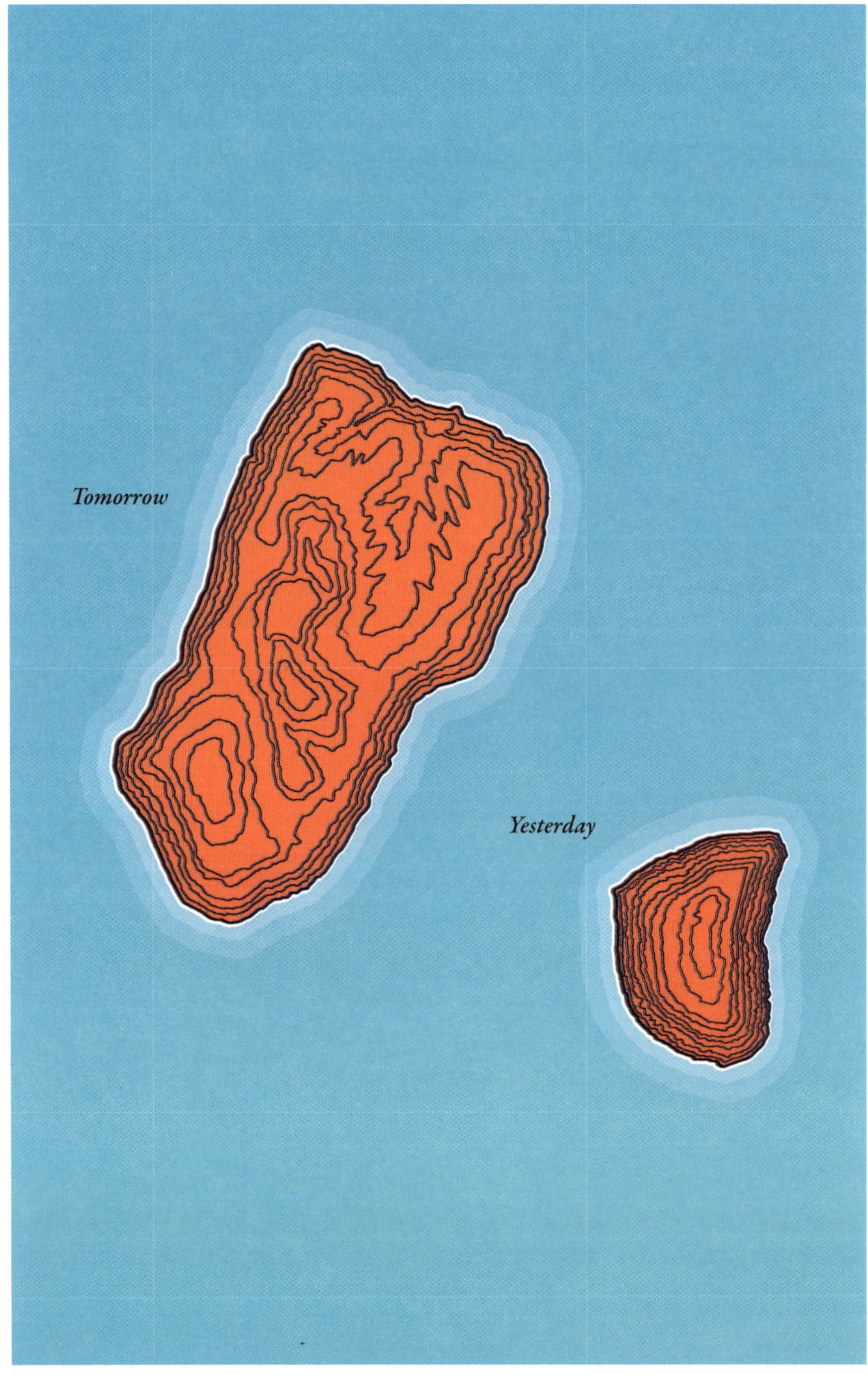
Tomorrow
Yesterday

YESTERDAY AND TOMORROW

A Cold War Across Time

YESTERDAY: COUNTRY United State of America **AREA** 6.3km^2 (2.4 square miles). **POPULATION** 80 permanent residents. **TOMORROW: COUNTRY** Russia **AREA** 29km^2 (11.2 square miles). **POPULATION** Zero permanent residents; patrolled by an unknown number of Russian border guards. **CHARACTERISTICS** Neighbouring islands that are a world apart. Also known as Little Diomede or Ignaluk and Big Diomede or Imaqliq, respectively, they are separated by politics and the International Date Line.

THIS IS WHERE RUSSIA and the USA come within kissing distance. A shade under 4 kilometres (2½ miles) of freezing water separate the two islands, each a citadel of sea cliffs, one Russian and the other American. They nudge noses in the Bering Strait, the icy passage that separates Alaska and Russia's Chukchi Peninsula. In the Iñupiat language they are called Inaliq ('the other one') and Imaqliq ('surrounded by water') but they are also commonly referred to as Yesterday and Tomorrow, because the International Date Line runs between them. This means that if you travelled from the Russian to the American island you would leap backwards one full day.

The remote regions that surround Yesterday and Tomorrow point to a shared history of colonial expansion. How did Russia, whose heartland is anchored over 6,000 kilometres (3,700 miles) to the west, and the USA, founded on the shore of another ocean 7,000 kilometres (4,350 miles) southeast of here, come to be winking at each other in the high Arctic? The story of Yesterday and Tomorrow is an intriguing parable of rivalry, conflict but also stupendous national enlargement.

Between Yesterday and Tomorrow we find the snowy cousin of the Iron Curtain that divided Europe from the Soviet bloc. It was called the Ice Curtain and ran between these islands. With the return of hostile relations in the 2010s it came back. The indigenous population who for millennia moved across this area without hindrance are more divided than ever.

The Iñupiat are a branch of the Inuit peoples and have been living on these islands for more than 3,000 years. Today they live only on Yesterday, in its one village, Inalik, which is huddled on a steep rocky patch on the island's western shore, which means the villagers always have a clear view of Russia. In 1990, 178 people lived here but today it has a population of 80 or so. It has a school, a church, a library and a heliport but there are no roads on the island and only one shop. Weather permitting, a weekly helicopter links it to the mainland. Yesterday is in decline and has an uncertain future. It's not hard to see why. It's about as remote as anywhere can be and the weather is brutal. Hunting is one of the few occupations available. Neither Yesterday or Tomorrow have trees and the only plants that thrive are low mosses and grasses though, in sheltered spots between rocks, you can find sourdock, mountain sorrel and a handful of other hardy flowering species. The one mammal found in the interior of the islands is the Artic fox, which eats ground-nesting birds and their eggs.

When the naturalist John Muir visited Inalik in 1881 he was not impressed. He called it among the 'dreariest towns I ever beheld':

> *The huts are mostly built of stone with skin roofs. They look like mere stoneheaps, black dots on the snow at a distance, with whalebones posts set up and framed at the top to lay their canoes beyond the dogs that would otherwise eat them.*

People who live in remote and extreme environments are often treated with a mixture of wonder and disdain. The bafflement endured by remote indigenous people is especially toxic in the Arctic, as it has led to the conviction that their forced relocation is some kind of favour. This is what happened on Tomorrow, which the Russians call Ostrov

Ratmanova (Ratmanova Island). The Iñupiat who once lived here were all forced to leave when the Soviet government built a military base on the island in 1948. Today there is only a weather station and some blocks for uniformed border guards.

What happened to the indigenous people of Tomorrow? It appears that some went east and joined their families in America while others moved to mainland Russia and assimilated. There was the occasional transgression of the Ice Curtain. One local historian writes that although 'officially forbidden to do so, Eskimos from the two sides did occasionally meet on the International Date Line under the cover of fog, visiting briefly, and exchanging small gifts'. But the drawing of a Cold War border between them, along with Soviet relocations, created an irrecoverable rift.

As the end of the Cold War approached in the 1980s, rapprochement was in the air. In 1987, the American swimmer Lynne Cox swam from Yesterday to Tomorrow accompanied in boats by most of the population of Yesterday, who wanted to get a closer look at the island of their kinfolk. It was a period of reconnection and outreach. In 1994, Inalik villagers made ready for the visit of about one hundred relatives from the east. Another breakthrough came when some Inalik residents travelled into the Russian province of Chukotka in search of family. 'By skis and dog sled we covered twenty to twenty-five miles a day and went to sixteen villages', one member of the expedition told a BBC reporter: 'I found relatives on my mother's side in three villages, and her favourite cousin – Luda – she was in Uelen. It was very special. I was with family again'.

The thaw was not to last. Political tensions returned and travel ground to a halt. Interviewed in 2015, Inalik resident Frances Ozenna explained that the search for lost kin was starting to seem fruitless: 'The thing is we know nothing about each other. We are losing our language. We speak English now and they speak Russian. It's not our fault. It's not their fault.' She dreams of a very different future: 'If we could get reunification going, it would bring a lot to our peace of minds here,' but adds, 'I don't think it's going to happen.'

Tribal leader Robert Soolook, who led the expedition to Chukotka, is also pessimistic. 'On the north side of the Russian island there's a military base,' he says, 'and when we're out hunting in the boat and get too close to the island they either send off a warning shot or holler at us telling us to go back.' Robert points out that 'We've been here for thousands of years, before the English came, the Americans, the Russians, before any governments and regulations separated us from our families. This border is breaking our hearts.'

Huge changes loom. The high Artic is seeing the steepest rises in temperature anywhere in the world and the prospect of a transpolar shipping route is very real. Once cargo vessels are able to cut straight across the North Pole, sailing from Asia to Europe, the Bering Strait may turn into an important shipping lane. Other plans include a tunnel under the Strait, linking the Americas and Asia. These tiny islands could find themselves transformed from places on the farthest margins to centre-stage.

Tunnel users would need to spin their watches twenty-four hours forwards or backwards depending on whether they are going east or west. Not a few will wonder why this awkward and dramatic transition happens here and not in the Atlantic or the English Channel? The answer is that when, in the 1880s, our current system of global time zones was developed, it was drawn up by Europeans who regarded the Pacific as an empty zone. They reasoned that it was the best place for the Date Line, since it would inconvenience the fewest number of people. However the transition towards the Bering Strait beoming a major transport hub is going to bring fresh scrutiny to that decision. With that scrutiny other questions will follow, such as why Russia and the USA touch toes in this distant land.

When the US bought Alaska from Russia in 1867 it got hold of an area twice the size of the thirteen original American colonies. Back then almost all Alaskans were indigenous Alaskans. Their claim on this land was not even considered when Russia sold it, nor were they consulted when, as part of the Alaska Purchase, an international border was drawn between the islands of Yesterday and Tomorrow. As so often in the story of islands, the people who live on them were invisible to the nations that decided their fate.

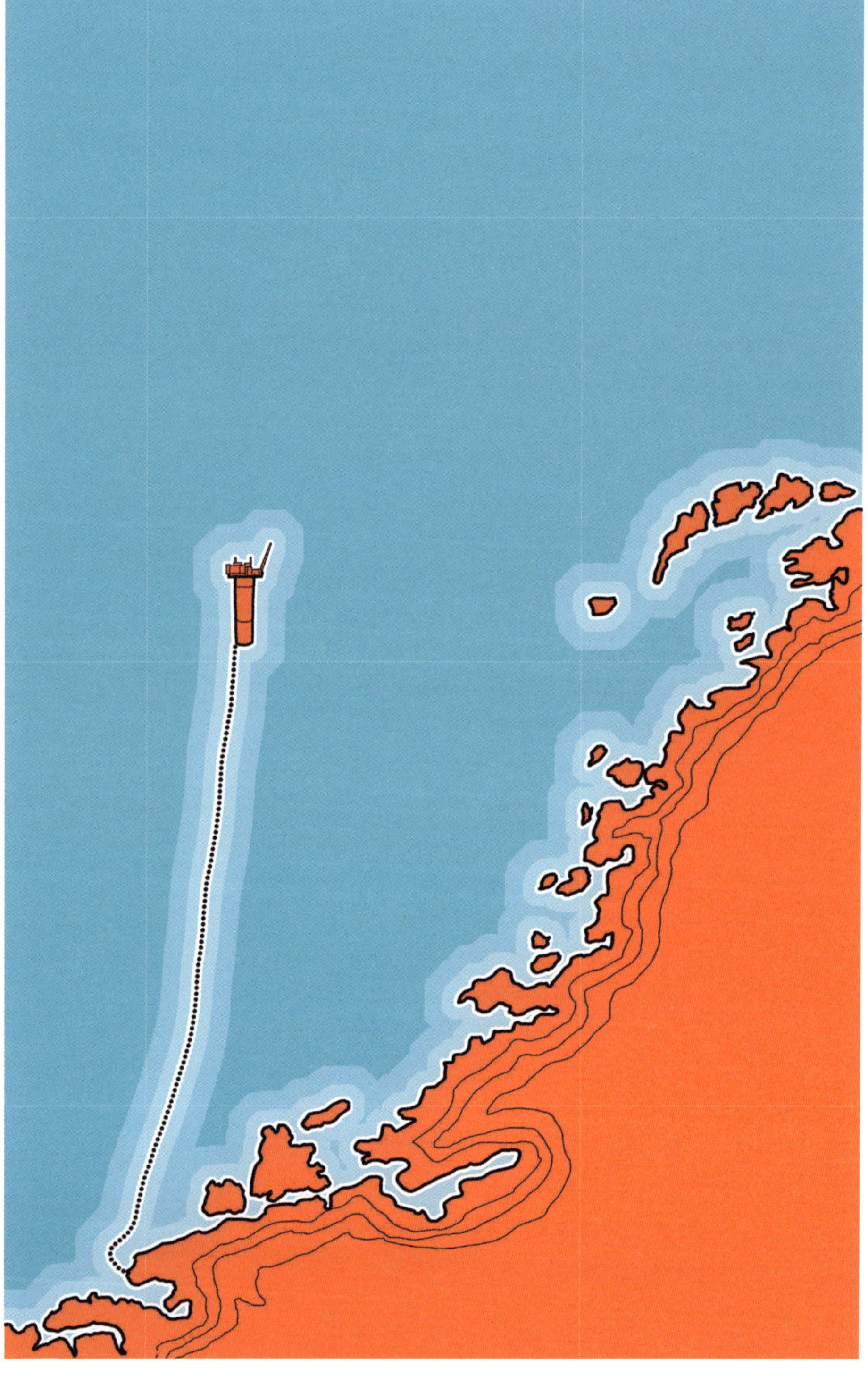

AASTA HANSTEEN

Mega Rigs at the Edge of the High Seas

COUNTRY Norway **AREA** 2,500m^2 (26,909ft^2). **POPULATION** Approximately 100.
CHARACTERISTICS A giant rig on the front line of Norway's push for additional marine territory in which to extract more oil and gas, in every way distant from its home country, which cultivates a green image.

THE HIGH SEAS belong to no nation. If you could find or fabricate an island in its deep waters it would be beyond the reach of any country's law. It looks like it's not going to be libertarian dreamers who will be the first to stake a claim but energy and mining companies. Giant rigs and giant drills are moving in. And which rapacious country is leading the pack? It's a land of clean air, pristine wilderness and lots of electric cars, somewhere that boasts it has the world's highest environmental and ethical values. It's a petro-state fox that dresses as a lamb: Norway.

Aasta Hansteen is a Norwegian floating gas rig that weighs 70,000 tonnes and, at 339 metres (1,112 feet), it is taller than the Eiffel Tower. It is tethered by chunky polyester cables to the seabed, which is over a kilometre down (1,200 metres/3,900 feet) and it can be found in icy seas beyond the Arctic Circle at the edge of Norway's 200-nautical-mile (370-kilometre) Exclusive Economic Zone. Apparently this is not enough to meet Norway's needs. It is pushing hard for this limit to be expanded and the whole undersea continental shelf (connected to both the Norwegian mainland and its scattered Arctic island possessions) to be awarded to its exclusive use and exploitation.

At the time of writing no rigs have crossed this threshold but Aasta Hansteen is scratching at the bars, a chained beast with the scent of oil and gas in its nostrils. It's an intoxicating aroma mixed with manganese, nickel, copper, cobalt, tellurium and rare earth elements. Once Norway's many-fanged mining machines are let slip they will swarm across the frontier; the seabed in the Atlantic's polar reaches will be gouged out and fresh fortunes will be made.

After a two-month journey from shipyards in South Korea, the main platform of Aasta Hansteen was carried by the world's largest heavy-transportation vessel and arrived in Norway in 2018. It's a floating village, with bedrooms and amenities for 108 workers. Access is by helicopter. The gas it extracts travels through a 482-kilometre- (300-mile-) long pipeline connected to the mainland. This pipeline was a huge investment and it is a tell-tale sign that Norway is banking on further discoveries around and beyond Aasta Hansteen.

This part of the Atlantic is divided into the Norwegian Sea, which is to the west of Norway and where Aasta Hansteen can be found, and the Barents Sea, which is to the north of mainland Norway. Dozens of new concessions for oil and gas exploitation have been granted across both. In 2024, the online news site *The Barents Observer* wryly observed that: 'Despite its commitment to cut climate gas emissions and reduce hydrocarbon dependence, Norway continues to expand exploration in the Barents Sea'. A more excited headline could be found in a mining news site called *Offshore Energy*: 'Norway goes on oil & gas spree and gives its blessing to projects worth over $18.5 billion'.

Norwegians do not need the money and the climate needs more fossil fuel production like a hole in the head. But Norwegians have convinced themselves that they are the good guys. In a gesture typical of this looking-glass world, both the rig and gas field the 'Aasta Hansteen' floats above are named after nineteenth-century Norwegian feminist, artist and author Aasta Hansteen, a woman who was famously poor, principled and implacable. One of the things Hansteen hated was avarice: 'Crush this money power!' she wrote, 'The human being is the most important thing.' The name 'Aasta Hansteen' has been co-opted to soft-sell hard-core greed. It's hard to imagine she would have been pleased but maybe her horror would allow a degree of fascination. Offshore rigs – Norway has built some of the largest – are sprouting like giant mushrooms off many coasts and they are colossal. Polar seas

have seen the creation of many innovative new islands, all built to access fossil fuels. There are 'sacrificial beach islands', 'rubble spray islands' and concrete and steel 'caisson islands'. Another variety is the ice island, which is fashioned from layers of frozen water and leaves the fewest scars on the landscape. However, in future years it will be the rigs that push beyond 200 nautical miles, into the High Seas, that will be making the news.

To understand the frontier nature of Aasta Hansteen we need to remind ourselves about the Law of the Sea. All countries have a 12-nautical-mile (22-kilometre) strip around their coast in which they can do what they want. The 200-nautical-mile (370-kilometre) Exclusive Economic Zone is an additional entitlement: an area in which nations have the exclusive right to exploit both the seabed and the 'water column': more simply, they can dig and fish. This zone extends from any land, so islands are highly valuable marine assets. The ideal island is a long way from anywhere: this gives its owning nation a 360-degree sweep of 200 nautical miles (370 kilometres). Norway is blessed with two such islands: Svalbard to the far north and Jan Mayeen. Jan Mayeen is about halfway between Norway and Greenland, 560 kilometres (around 350 miles) north of Iceland and populated by a dozen or so staff from the Norwegian Army and Norwegian Meteorological Institute. Jan Mayeen is a desolate mountain in the middle of nowhere but it gifts Norway a vast stretch of exploitable ocean.

Norway's Exclusive Economic Zone (EEZ) amounts to 2,385,178 square kilometres (920,922 square miles). It's claiming more and is able to do so because the international law on who owns what at sea is tilted in the favour of those with the sharpest legal elbows. The United Nations Convention on the Law of the Sea made a ruling in 1982 that gave nations EEZs but also 'continental shelf rights'. According to the Convention a continental shelf may not extend beyond 350 nautical miles (648 kilometres) or, alternatively, more than 100 nautical miles (185 kilometres) beyond the point at which the seabed lies at a depth of 2,500 metres (8,200 feet). Since 2009, Norway has been pushing hard and successfully to have its continental shelf rights recognized.

None of this mattered when there were enough minerals on land or near to the shore. But there is a growing demand for the metals that go into new tech devices like smartphones, and sanctions against Russia have pinched supply. The negative consequences of the 1982 UN ruling, with its generous provision of rights, are becoming clear. Rather than treating the oceans as a shared treasure, the so-called 'Law of the Sea' has become a recipe for exploitation – and conflict. Disagreements about where shelves are and where they end are now common. Norway and Russia have overlapping continental shelf claims and neither wants to back down.

The fact that rich Norway has positioned itself as the standard bearer of a new wave of undersea exploitation is setting a precedent. Why should much poorer nations hold back? Professor Rak Kim, of the Copernicus Institute of Sustainable Development, at Utrecht University, explains that Norway's actions are a 'disappointment ... not because of the immediate impact that exploration might have, but it changes the political dynamic'.

Aasta Hansteen and other rigs are far out to sea. No one can see them and this has helped them evade public scrutiny or awareness. How else to explain the fact that Norway can be both a petro-state and cast itself as an environmentalist beacon? There is a kind of grim humour in the tourist branding of Norway as a destination for lovers of unspoilt nature. In 2024 there was a survey designed to find Europe's greenest country. The winner? 'Norway takes the crown'. Of course it does. The awarding panel was impressed by the fact the Norwegian government is 'dedicated to reaching net-zero carbon emissions' and has 'pledged up to three billion Norwegian Krone per year to help save tropical forests around the world'. That's not all: 'Norway's capital, Oslo, is also a notably eco-friendly city, with lots of green policies to protect its nature'. It's a long way from Oslo to the endlessly churning, spinning drills of Aasta Hansteen and its kin, the monsters that keep the kroner rolling in and that, day and night, prowl Norway's expanding outer limits.

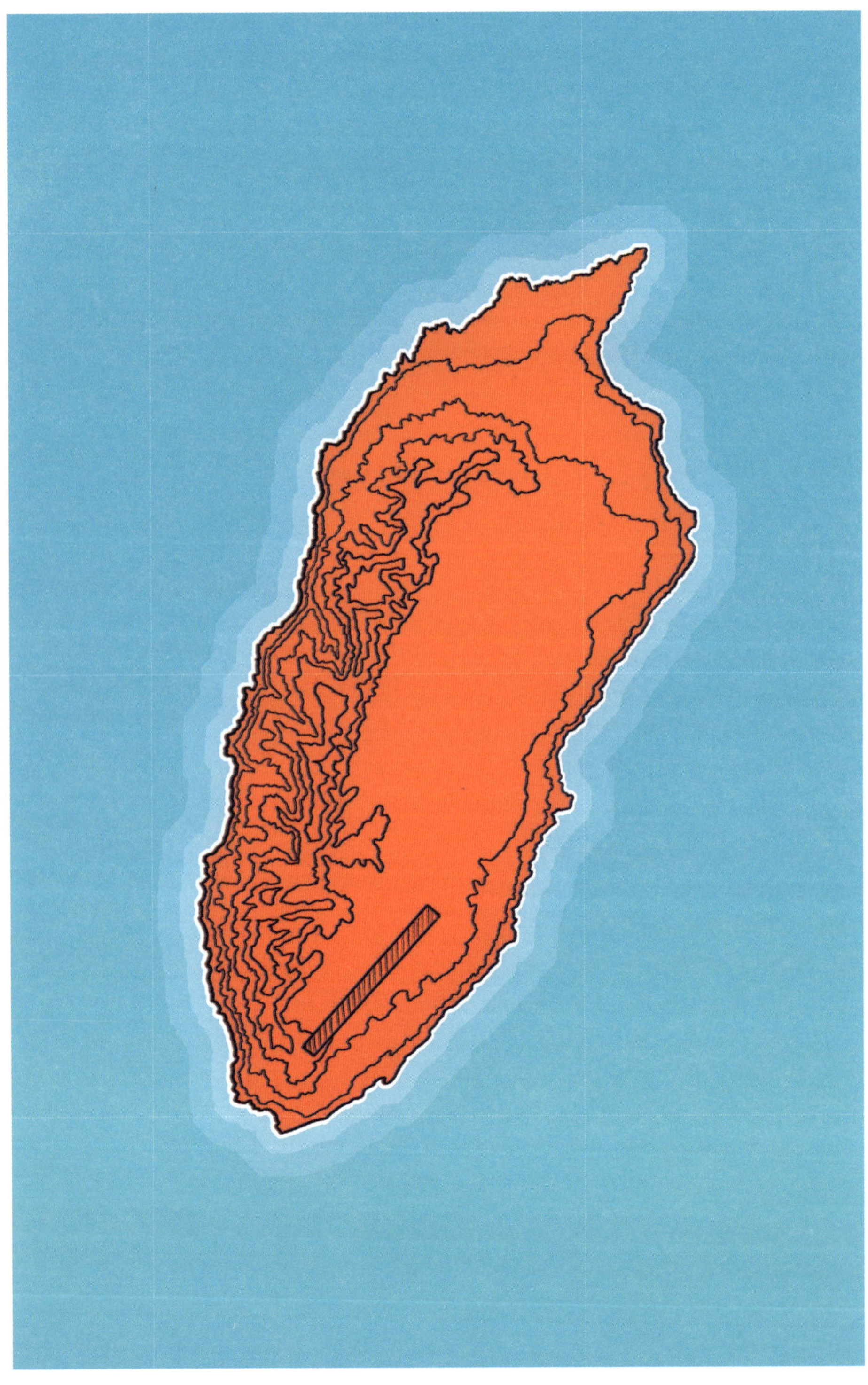

SAN NICOLAS ISLAND

A Story of Survival and Loss

COUNTRY United States of America **AREA** 58.93km² (22.7 square miles). **POPULATION** Approximately 200 (military and civilian). **CHARACTERISTICS** Home of the sole survivor of the indigenous people who had lived on this rocky Californian island for millennia; she became known as the 'Lone Woman of San Nicolas Island'.

THIS IS A TALE OF ENDURANCE and isolation on a faraway island but it is also about you and me, and about why we see our reflection in lonely survivors.

San Nicolas Island is 98 kilometres (61 miles) from the southern California coast. It's an arid sandstone island and the most distant of California's Channel Islands. It has been inhabited for thousands of years and has more than 540 archaeological sites. Today it is run by the United States Navy, which uses it for weapons testing and training, and it is off-limits to the public. It is famous as the home of the Lone Woman of San Nicolas, a Native American woman who was the island's sole inhabitant from 1835 until 1853; the last survivor of the island's indigenous people and the last speaker of their language. Nearly all her kin had been massacred by hunters working for Russian traders and her legend soon spread. In 1852 a Santa Barbara rancher went in search of the Lone Woman and found footprints. He came back and discovered her living in a whalebone hut, skinning a seal. 'The old woman was of medium height but rather thick,' he wrote, adding, 'she must have been about 50 years old but she was still strong and active. Her face was pleasing, as she was continuously smiling. Her teeth were entire but worn to the gums.' The 'Lone Woman' shared some roasted roots with the newcomer, who persuaded her to come back to Santa Barbara.

Through sign language the Lone Woman communicated she had stayed on the island because her baby son was there. He grew up on the island but appears to have been killed by a whale or shark as a young man. A few months after her rescue, and apparently unable to cope with the rich diet on the mainland, the Lone Woman died of dysentery. On her deathbed, she was baptized and given the name Juana Maria.

The Lone Woman's lonely end added further allure to her story. From the mid-nineteenth century, narratives of indigenous people as noble yet doomed were beginning to make sad stories like hers attractive to urban Americans and, when combined with her similarity to Robinson Crusoe, the world's best-known castaway, the legend of the Lone Woman became irresistible. Media interest can be traced from the 1840s onwards and it has never really let up. One of the oldest news items is from an 1847 edition of *The Boston Daily Atlas* and is headlined 'A FEMALE CRUSOE'. The story is prefaced with a description of the Lone Woman's tribe as 'a listless, quiet race of beings' who, this reporter tells us, fell victim to 'a party of Kodiac Indians' who spread 'disease and contention' among the island's 'unsuspecting and unsophisticated inhabitants'. A handful of survivors were taken to the mainland but the Lone Woman jumped ship: she 'plunged into the abyss' says the Boston paper and 'in another moment, stood alone on the shores of her native land' then 'disappeared forever from the sight of her astonished and sorrowing companions'.

This account set a tone that, over the following decades, has not been much deviated from: each retelling maintaining the idea that this is a tragic but also a thrilling tale, a story of loss but also of stoic and glorious independence. There she still is, wrote the awe-struck reporter:

The monarch of all she surveys. She preferred to part even with her chosen mate and sever every human tie that could be binding, rather than leave the home of her birth – that lonely little Isle, that had been to her a world, which she cared not to exchange for the abode of civilized man, with all its promised luxuries.

A digital archive has been created detailing all the newspaper articles about the Lone Woman: they are usually low-key, back-page stuff but they have been sustained across an extraordinarily long period of time. Her curious tale appears to be infinitely repeatable. Perhaps this is because the Lone Woman is both exotic and relatable: her unknown language and her lost tribe have a ghostly fascination, a defanged reminder of the violence of colonization, yet her Boy Scout ingenuity, cobbling together shelter and sustenance on her own little patch, make her into a very domestic sort of stranger, an adventurous, unfamiliar version of ourselves.

The Lone Woman's story went from curio to mainstream when it was discovered by the novelist Scott O'Dell, who turned it into one of America's most-loved children's books, *Island of the Blue Dolphins*, which was published in 1960, and inspired a film a few years later. The Lone Woman became 'Karana' and O'Dell recounts some key aspects of her real-life story. One of the ways that O'Dell made the Lone Woman appealing was by emphasizing that she was 'at one' with nature. In his telling, the moment she decided to return to the island, dolphins leap in front her, offering her cheer and company. Another device O'Dell made use of comes straight from the pages of Daniel Defoe's *Robinson Crusoe,* which owes much of its enduring popularity to its detailed, first-person accounts of food gathering and home making. O'Dell does the same for Karana. One of her first tasks was to create a shelter, not so easy on an island with few trees. She makes use of large whale bones: 'I put the ribs together with their edges almost touching', O'Dell writes, and between them 'I wove many strands of bull kelp, which shrinks as it dries and pulls very tight', and for a door 'I covered the hole with a mat woven of brush to shed the rain'.

The whalebone hut was built by the real Lone Woman but it had long been recorded that her real home was a cave. For years no one could find it. This was to change in the 2010s when United States Navy archaeologist Steve Schwartz, who had spent twenty years looking for the cave, announced a new discovery. He had found an 1879 map of the island with an 'Indian Cave' identified and, after exploring the area numerous times, one day Schwartz noticed a ridge of rock jutting from a low cliff. He guessed there might be something underneath the ridge

– something now buried by sand. After digging down through metres of infill his hunch proved right. It's a long cavern, at least 23 metres (75 feet) long and 3 metres (10 feet) high, and it seems that a hundred years ago tourists had already visited, for two sets of chiselled graffiti initials and dates were found just inside the cave entrance, both from 1911. Two redwood boxes were also found not far away, apparently made from canoe planks, containing 200 stone blades, harpoon points, bone fishhooks and other implements. It is likely these were the Lone Woman's, both because they are contemporaneous with her time on the island and because she was known to have stashed useful items.

New finds keep interest in the Lone Woman alive and the focus on her as a sole survivor keeps the story simple. But it also means her tribe and her partner, the father of her baby, is forgotten. It's interesting that, in *The Boston Daily Atlas* story from 1847, he is as prominent as she is. It's easy to see why: his tale is just as poignant and even more sad. Having been put ashore on a mainland beach he refused to leave, staring out to sea, apparently bereft: 'Alone and friendless, there he remained', the Boston paper tells us, 'an isolated being, till life ceased to animate his frame'. He kept this vigil going for many months: 'a solitary outcast' watching sunset and sunrise, 'with his eyes gazing on that celestial orb as it sank into the western horizon, a direction which he well knew pointed to the lost but never forgotten home of his nativity'. After two years this Lone Man was found dead on the strand: 'a stiffened corse [corpse], stretched out, and bleaching, as it were, in the white foam on the surf, which was thrown about his lifeless remains as the mighty wave broke on the shore'.

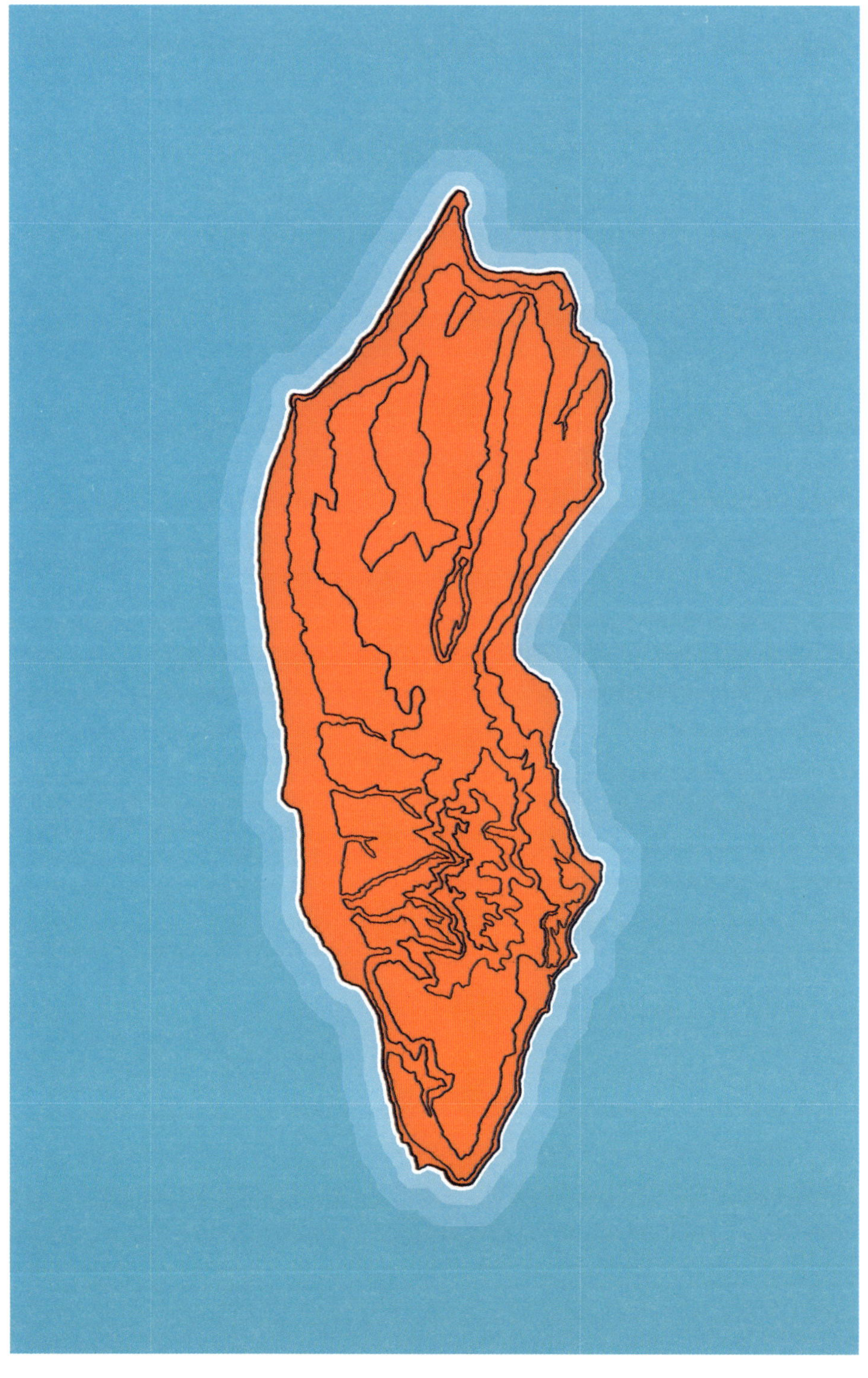

SOCOTRA

Dragon Blood Trees and Fighter Jets

COUNTRY Yemen **AREA** 3,796km² (1,466 square miles). **POPULATION** Approximately 60,000. **CHARACTERISTICS** An arid, mountainous and remote island famous for its unique plant life and culture, coveted for its geopolitical position.

NATURAL WONDER OR STRATEGIC military base? Socotra is both. It is about 340 kilometres (210 miles) from Yemen's coast and has an unmatched proportion of endemic (unique) species but it is also in a military hot spot; airstrips now scar its rocky surface.

Socotra is about 134 kilometres (83 miles) long and up to 40 kilometres (25 miles) wide. It is arid and mountainous, its highest peak rising to 1,500 metres (4,900 feet). Three much smaller islands and a couple of rocky islets form the Socotra archipelago. Isolation helps explain the emergence of the island's bizarre and striking flora. The island's iconic dragon blood tree (*Dracaena cinnabari*) is named after its red sap, which is used as a dye – by violinmakers, for example, including Antonio Stradivari – and has been traded since Roman times. The dragon blood tree grows up to 9 metres (30 feet) tall and above its tangle of branches sits a neat leafy dome, making the tree look like a fat green umbrella. There are said to be about 900,000 or so of these trees left on the island, but climate change means that there are few new saplings and the bones of dead dragons have become a common sight.

Over a third of the island's plants are unique to Socotra. The increasingly rare Socotra desert rose (*Adenium socotranum*) is a bulbous succulent that produces brilliant pink and red flowers. It has evolved to store water in its swollen limbs, allowing it to survive extended periods of drought. Another species for which the island is famed is the olibanum tree (*Boswellia sacra*). The tree is not unique to Socotra, but its sap produces frankincense, and Socotra's specimens are said to offer the world's finest. In addition to its distinctive plants, it has been estimated that 90 per cent of Socotra's reptile species and 95 per cent of its snails do not occur anywhere else in the world. The island also supports globally significant populations of land and sea birds and around its shores live a wonderful array of marine life, including 300 species of crab, lobster and shrimp, 253 species of coral and 730 species of coastal fish.

In 2008, Socotra was recognized as a UNESCO World Heritage Site, the UN committee declaring that it was 'one of the most biodiversity rich and distinct islands in the world'. The UN designation was based on more than an appreciation of the island's natural heritage – it also refers to its cultural heritage. Socotra's 60,000 or so people are part of what makes the island special. UNESCO tells us they have 'co-existed with this rich natural environment and been its careful guardians'. The UN experts point to the islanders' traditions of sustainable herding for goats, sheep, cattle and camels. In such a dry place, nature's bounty cannot be squandered. The island's plants have been protected by the Socotrans, and the plants in turn have established microclimates that conserve water and prevent the erosion of the thin soils. Traditionally, the islanders harvested wood, fibres, leaves and fruit, without damaging the island's fragile ecosystems; this harvest has been the mainstay of their daily economy, being used to make everything from rope to medicine, as well as dyes, adhesives, pesticides, fertilizers, cosmetics and toys.

The singularity of Socotra spills in many directions. The island has its own language, Soqotri, which has a variety of dialects. But with no written form and no official status, like many other aspects of the island's ancient character, Soqotri is endangered. Arabic, which is the language of government as well as schooling, radio and television, is now replacing it.

Socotra is a unique place but, increasingly, outsiders see its special character not in terms of its flora, fauna or human culture but in its location. This has happened before. Back when a communist regime was in charge in South Yemen (it was the Arab world's only communist state, which survived from 1967 until 1990), the Soviet Union used Socotra as an anchorage for ships and submarines. Today the island is officially and supposedly under the control of Yemen's internationally

recognized government, which is called the Presidential Leadership Council, and based in exile in Riyadh, the capital of Saudi Arabia. The Presidential Leadership Council is backed by Saudi Arabia as well as the West and locked in combat with the Iranian-backed Houthi forces that control much of western Yemen.

Yemen is a broken country and its power over Socotra is weak. The country with the biggest sway over the island appears to be the United Arab Emirates (UAE), which backs another faction fighting the Houthis, the Southern Transitional Council, which claims to represent southern Yemenis, including the Socotrans. The UAE is a small country, but it has deep pockets and it is using its leverage over the Yemenis to turn Socotra into a kind of colony. It's easy to see why Socotra matters to the region's geopolitical strategists. It sits at the bottom of the Arabian Peninsula, between the Gulf of Aden and the Gulf of Oman, and it is a key asset in securing and projecting power across the region. From a UAE perspective, it is more protector than predator. About 30 per cent of Socotrans live in the UAE and at least some Socotrans welcome the stability and money the Emiratis bring.

Socotra has been spared the violence of the Yemen civil war, but it is adrift and unguarded, a situation that was exacerbated in the 2010s by storms that destroyed much of its infrastructure, as well as thousands of its unique trees. It was in the aftermath of the devastation that the geopolitical gaming of the island began in earnest. First the Emiratis stepped in: on 30 April 2018, a hundred UAE soldiers turned up, apparently without any warning or consultation. Soon workers arrived to rebuild the port, and construct a water network, educational and health facilities. The official UAE line was that they were there to improve 'stability, health care, education and living conditions'.

Yemen's Presidential Leadership Council declared it was an act of aggression. A standoff ensued, with Saudi Arabia acting as an interested mediator. The UAE troops eventually left; and Saudi forces arrived, also promising aid and development. In 2020 the tables turned again, and the Saudis left. The Southern Transitional Council appears to have invited the Emiratis back in. A 2021 press report stated that the UAE was, once again, in control, and was now paying the salaries of civil servants on the island, and flying the UAE flag at police checkpoints.

In 2024, a satellite photo of one of Socotra's minor islands, Abd al-Kuri Island, showed the construction of a new airstrip and the words 'I LOVE UAE' ploughed into the ground next to the runway. Is the UAE here to stay? Socotrans wish they knew. They find themselves in the midst of a four-way negotiation, which sometimes looks like a tussle, that is taking place over their heads. It is between the Presidential Leadership Council, the Southern Transitional Council, the UAE and Saudi Arabia. Complicated as that sounds, the reality is even murkier. In 2022 the Southern Transitional Council threw in its lot with the Presidential Leadership Council – and the UAE and Saudi Arabia act separately but also coordinate. For islanders it must be very confusing. However, they know one thing –whoever is in charge, it is not them.

There are many islands that have a strategic location. The real uniqueness of Socotra lies in its natural and cultural heritage but amid the political turmoil, environmental protection is no longer a priority. According to Muslim Climate Watch, a charity based in Washington, D.C., 'funding for environmental protection has dried up, leaving native initiatives to save the Dragon Blood tree languishing'. They also note that the headquarters of a powerful force for good on the island, the Socotra Environmental Protection Authority, has been converted into a military base.

Let's hope that one day the civil war ends, the soldiers move out and the conservationists move back in. Socotra is one of the most extraordinary islands in the world. It is a unique place. Its people and its curious plants and trees should be left in peace.

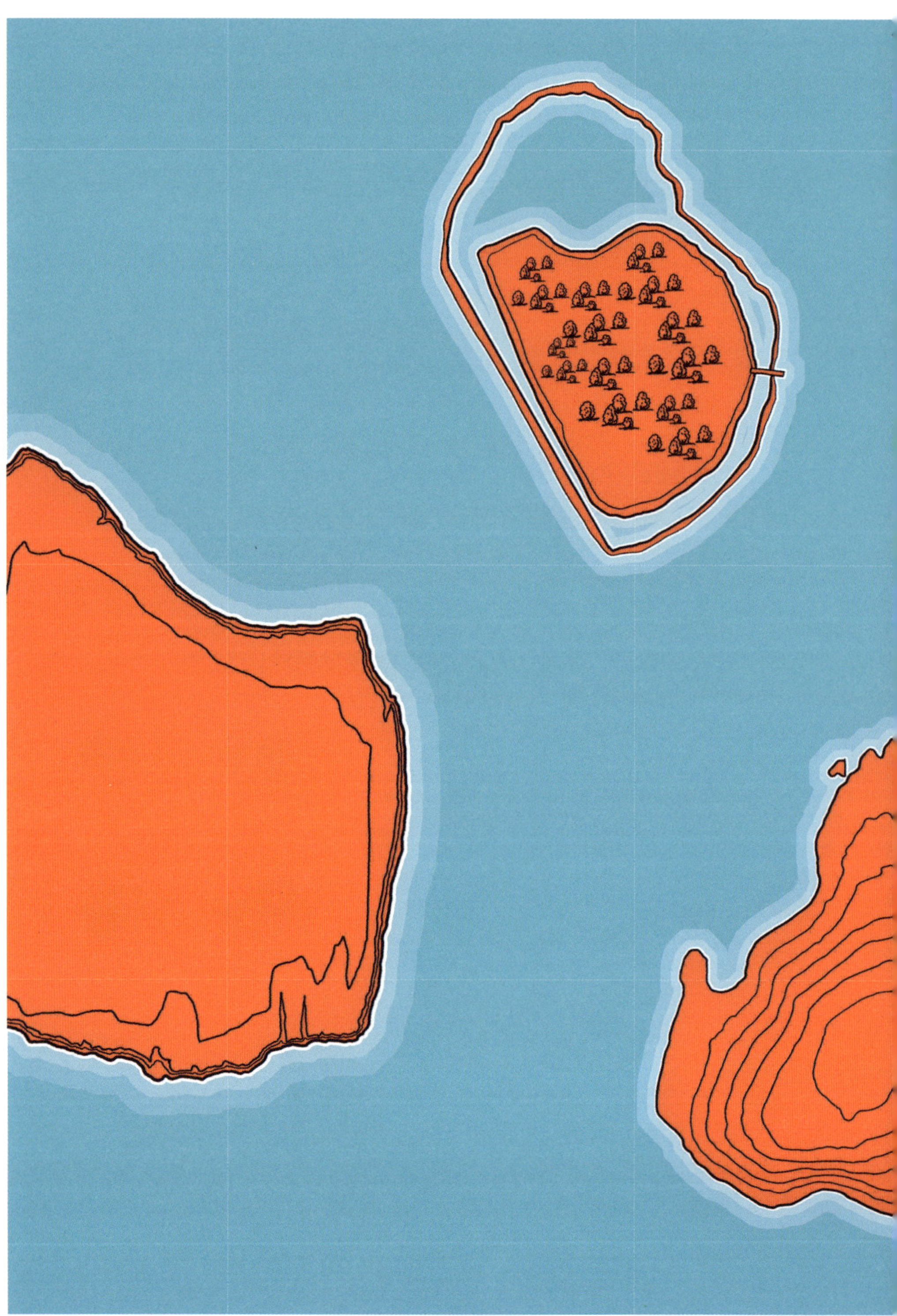

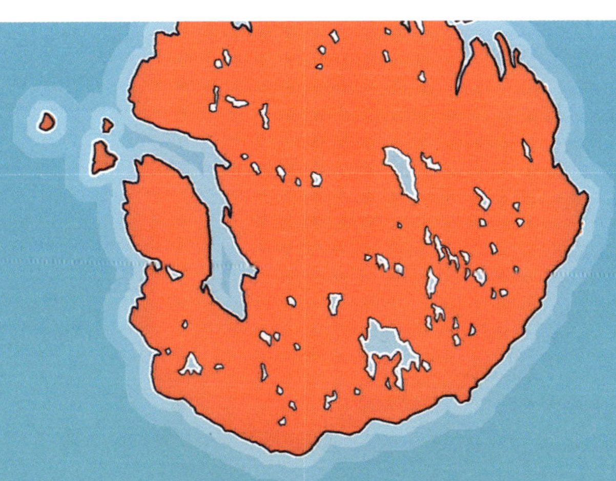

NATURALLY ODD ISLANDS

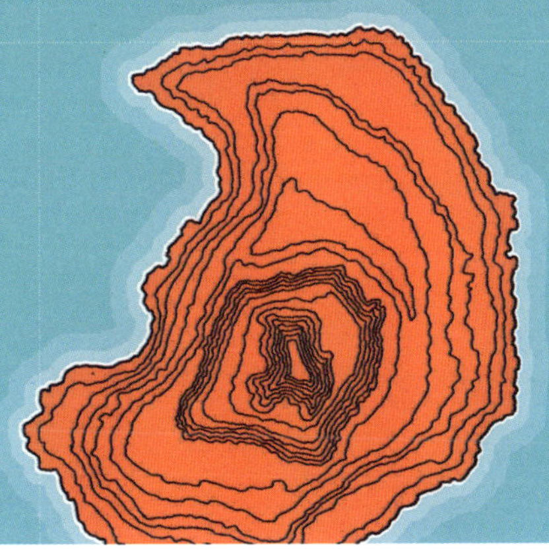

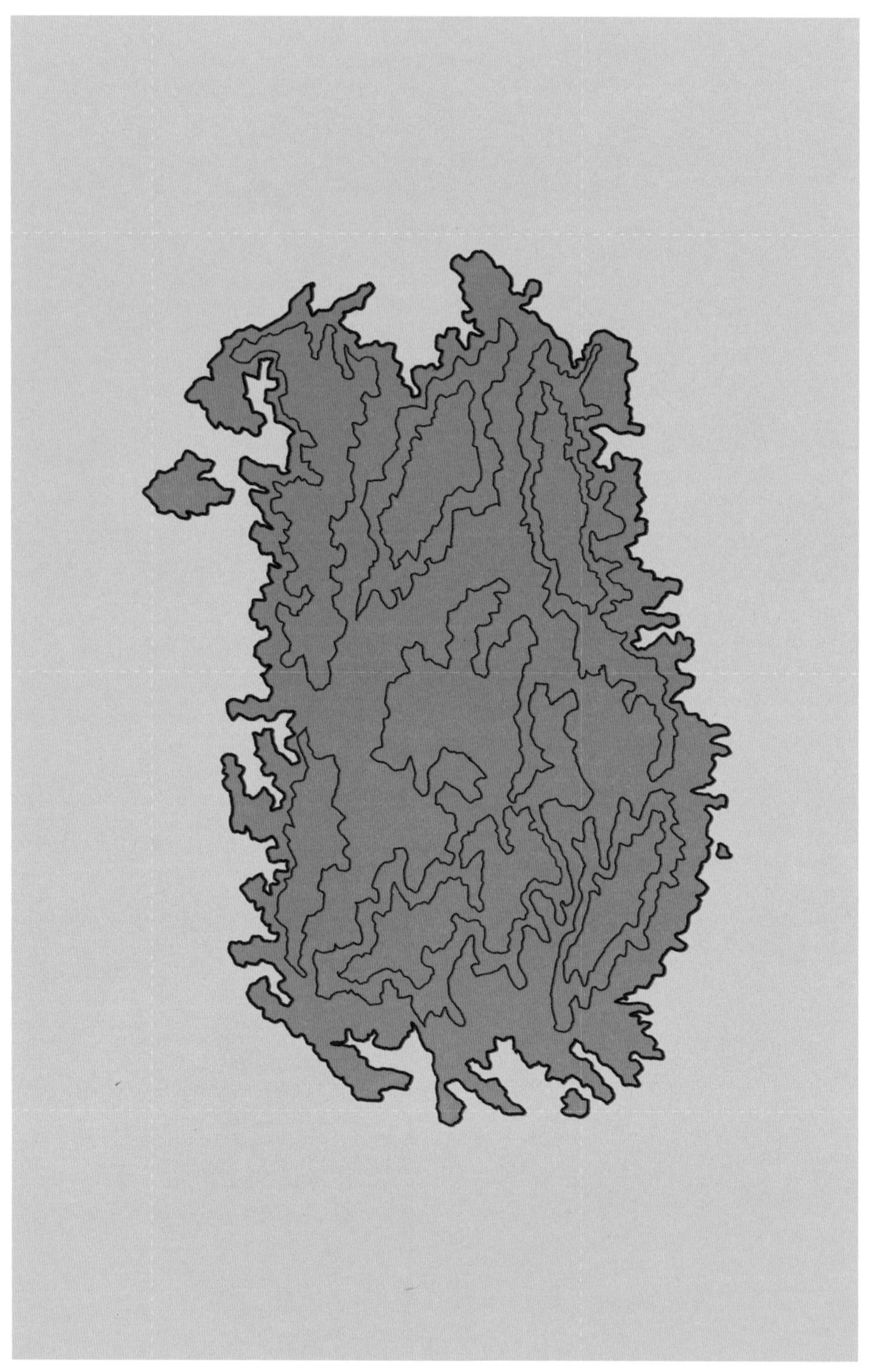

MAYDA INSULA AND THE MAGIC ISLANDS OF TITAN

Extraterrestrial Shores

LOCATION Titan, moon of Saturn **AREA** Observed as 260km^2 (100 square miles). **POPULATION** Unknown. **CHARACTERISTICS** Islands found on a lake on Titan; the more we learn about them the more extraordinary they appear.

THE DISCOVERY OF the first extraterrestrial islands is an important moment. The stuff of Earth – beaches, flowing rivers, clear lakes, wonderful islands – can all be found on Titan, the largest moon of Saturn. We have been waiting for life on other planets for so long, wondering and worrying about discovering something, anything, that could be called living, that the significance of this discovery has been overlooked. It may not be life but it is a recognizable landscape. Earth has found a cousin, a very strange cousin, but family.

Titan has a network of lakes, the largest being Kraken Mare and Ligeia Mare, that are not unlike the Great Lakes of North America, though much larger, and they are dotted with islands. Mayda Insula, the first named extraterrestrial island, is in Kraken Mare, the largest lake in the solar system (it is about the size of the Black Sea). Mayda Insula was named after a phantom island that early map-makers mistakenly thought existed somewhere in the North Atlantic. It's oval shaped, with lots of rocky coves and peninsulas. At 150 kilometres (93 miles) in length and 90 kilometres (56 miles) in width it's about the same size as the Balkan country of Montenegro.

So far just one spacecraft has landed on Titan, a long way south of the lakes, so all we know of Mayda Insula has been worked out from distant images. It has hills and valleys, all composed of the same orange-tinged rock and sand that is found across Titan and its highest point is 1,200 metres (just over 3,900 feet) above lake level. Radar images also reveal erosion on Mayda Insula's coast, with sediments carried along the shores of Kraken Mare. We know so little but what we do know is tantalizing: simultaneously familiar and unfamiliar. It's not even certain yet that Mayda Insula is a proper island; it may be joined to the mainland by a narrow neck of land, or it may even alternate between the two states.

Since the discovery of Mayda Insula another thirteen islands have been identified in Titan's lakes. The lakes look orange and clear, reflecting the Titan atmosphere, but rather than water are made of liquid methane and ethane at a temperature of around -180°C (-292°F). Titan has a thick atmosphere, a golden shroud of nitrogen and methane, and it also has evaporation, clouds and rainfall; similar to a complete hydrological cycle, but none of this is water. Even waves on these giant lakes look strange. The gap between each one is uncannily long, a phenomenon that has been attributed to Titan's very low gravity. Titan is a looking-glass world: recognizable yet alien.

Geography is no longer only an earth science. It has found a new shore and meteorologists as well as oceanographers are rewriting their textbooks. This revolution was begun by the tireless work of Cassini, the spacecraft that explored Saturn and its moons from 2004 all the way to 2017. It dropped the Huygens probe that landed on the surface of Titan in 2005. During its descent it sent back pictures of river channels and shores. It survived 1 hour and 12 minutes on the planet's surface, capturing extraordinary images of a forbidding and rocky landscape, images tinged with Titan's characteristic orange haze.

Both Kraken Mare and Ligeia Mare also have 'magic islands'. This is the name scientists used when they first spotted these mysterious and unmappable features, and it seems to have stuck. The most studied one is in Ligeia Mare: a 260-square-kilometre (100-square-mile) island that comes and goes, rises and falls, sometimes over weeks, sometimes in a matter of hours. It's been a source of debate and consternation.

Let's remind ourselves that Titan is 1.2 billion kilometres (746 million miles) away from Earth, many times more distant than the Sun. There is ample excuse for ignorance as well as huge scope for speculation. It has been suggested that the 'magic islands' could be visual anomalies in the imaging process, or reflections on the lake surface. An international team of scientists looked at these 'anomalous, bright features' and decided they were real – there is some *thing* there – but they were hesitant about jumping to conclusions. The 'islands' could be 'waves, rising bubbles, and suspended and/or floating solids' they wrote, concluding that current data does not allow us to 'discard any of these hypotheses'. However in 2024 a fresh study was undertaken that counters the 'waves' and 'rising bubbles' theories, along with the idea that the islands are ice that rises then melts. University of Texas planetary scientist Xinting Yu used sophisticated models of the Titan atmosphere to propose that the islands are something like snow, which falls from the sky and floats for a while before filling with liquid and sinking. Yu and her co-authors argue that most of the precipitation in Titan 'would land as solids' and that when these 'solids' settle on the lake they form into temporary islands. 'Imagine a sponge, full of holes', she says ...

If the solids are like this, with twenty-five to sixty per cent of their volume being empty space, they can float. Some solids, like hydrogen cyanide ice, can also float due to surface tension effects. If these conditions are not met, they sink into the lake liquids, adding to the lakebed sediments ... our study suggests that the magic islands might be made of large chunks of porous organic solids.

It's a working hypothesis. Theories and visions are swarming round Titan. It's easy to see why. There are 150 moons in our solar system, but Titan is special. It is the most Earth-like planet we know. The desire to recognize it as a home-from-home is powerful. What gets people really excited is Titan's deadly chemical mix. Its lakes are sea-sized reservoirs of liquid methane. Methane burns: it's fuel and it has been estimated that the lakes contain about 300 times the volume of Earth's proven oil reserves. Titan also has huge dunes of granular hydrocarbons. According to Ralph Lorenz, one of the scientists currently studying Titan, it is 'just covered in carbon-bearing material – it's a mega factory of organic chemicals'. The abundant nitrogen in the atmosphere could also be useful, especially in making fertilizer. And deep beneath its icy shell Titan has a trump card: it is thought that Titan has a huge subsurface ocean of water several times larger than all the oceans of Earth.

Titan may be in pole position for long-term human colonization. Robert Zubrin, an aerospace engineer who has long argued for the colonization of Mars, is a big fan of Titan. 'In certain ways,' he says, 'Titan is the most hospitable extraterrestrial world within our solar system for human colonization.'

Any colonizer would feel the weight of Titan's thick atmosphere. All that cloud and gas means that atmospheric pressure is about 60 per cent heavier than on Earth. Being a small planet, however, it also has low gravity. This unique ratio of atmospheric density and low surface gravity means that getting around on Titan would be easier than on Earth. In his techno-utopian treatise *Entering Space: Creating a Spacefaring Civilization*, Zubrin claims that anyone could take a pair of wings and fly across Titan's surface. There is a problem: it would take years to get to Titan. One of the most exciting space missions planned for the next few decades will see a return to Titan. NASA's Dragonfly spacecraft is due to launch in 2028 and will arrive six years later. It will position a robotic-flight-capable vehicle on Titan's surface, a rotor machine able to travel at about 36 kilometres (22 miles) per hour and fly up to an altitude of 4 kilometres (2½ miles). One of Dragonfly's aims is to investigate the potential for human colonization. It also wants to find out if the planet's hydrocarbons reveal any of the chemical building blocks of life.

NASA's Dragonfly is a new type of space mission, focused on 'astrobiology', the meeting point of the science of carbon, the science of life and space exploration. What will it find? Hopefully, one morning, in 2034, we'll wake up to find out.

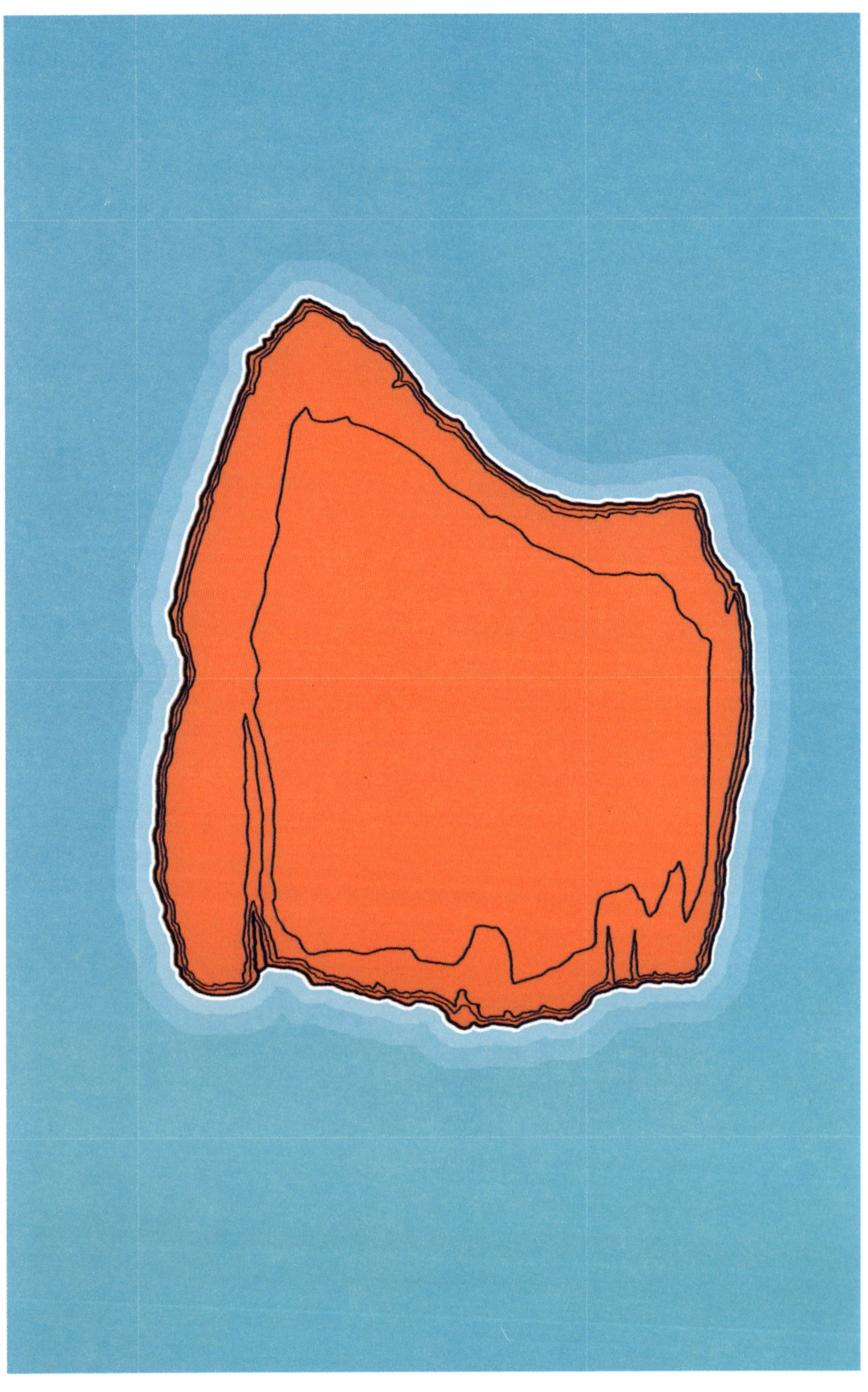

A23a

A Travelling Island

COUNTRY None **AREA** Changeable. In 2024, 4,000km² (1,500 square miles) **POPULATION** Zero. **CHARACTERISTICS** A huge iceberg that broke away from Antarctica. Sometimes grounded, sometimes spinning, sometimes sailing free, its movements have been closely watched by scientists.

ICEBERGS CAN BE the size of countries and as they drift and splinter, they reshape continents. In 2024 A23a was a couple of hundred metres thick and a rectangle of ice about half the size of Crete. Its flat top and steep size meant that, like all supersize icebergs, it is what is called a tabular iceberg. Smaller ones can be all shapes and sizes, and are often peaked like little mountains, but the big ones are slabs. A23a was a child of the south, carving off from an even more massive block that itself carved off from the Filchner Ice Shelf in Antarctica in 1986. Back then the Soviet Union's Druzhnaya research station was on this Antarctic edge. Its new situation, on a fragmenting and mobile island, was terrifying and Druzhnaya's buildings and equipment were airlifted to another site.

A23a floated north but became stranded, grounded by its own massive weight on the floor of the Weddell Sea. It remained like this, a beached ice island, for decades. Icebergs don't just bob about like bathtub toys: they often get stuck on the seabed, and they plough the seafloor in a process called iceberg scouring. As they grind along, plants and animals, such as seagrasses and molluscs, are crushed, releasing tonnes of stored carbon. But Antarctic icebergs are a source of life as well as a cause of death. When they melt, they release mineral-rich dust picked up in their youth, when they were part of a glacier rasping along the rocky valleys of Antarctica. When this dust is released into the ocean it becomes a source of nutrients for the plankton that are the basic building block of the marine food chain.

Lorna Linch, a lecturer in physical geography at the University of Brighton, explains that icebergs can trail good news: 'There is an increase in organism growth and levels of chlorophyll (the green pigment in plants used for photosynthesis) in the surrounding water', she tells us, and this 'can result in vibrant blooms that extract millions of tonnes of CO_2 from the atmosphere as they grow'. These 'blooms' can be ten times the length of the iceberg and last for about a month.

The destiny of all icebergs that are released into the open sea is oblivion. Anchored to the ocean floor for decades, in 2023 A23a had shed enough weight to be on the move again. It lumbered north towards Elephant Island, a proboscis-shaped island a few hundred kilometres from Antarctica. As it journeyed, research drones swooped around A23a's magnificent bulk, most of which was hidden under the water (roughly 90 per cent of an iceberg is below the water line). A magical ice kingdom was revealed: warmer waters sculpted leaping arches and large blue caverns.

The remarkable arches and caves of the world's biggest iceberg briefly caught the attention of the world press, as did its eccentric movements. In early 2024, A23a drifted over an underwater mountain, a seamount. Currents hitting the seamount created a vortex of water that hooked on to A23a, causing it to spin. A23a was, as Alexander Brearley, an oceanographer from the British Antarctic Survey, explained, 'basically just sitting there, spinning around and it will very slowly melt as long as it stays there'. Later the same year A23a broke free, heading off to find its grave in the Atlantic.

Large tabular icebergs regularly make their stately way up the Southern Ocean and become grounded off isolated islands. There is nothing new in this procession and giant bergs have been breaking off ice sheets for millions of years. The difference is that today they are doing so more often. The great ice shelves at both poles are in danger of collapse. A23 and A23a's dashes for freedom were part of a mass breakout from the Filchner Ice Shelf and became key exhibits in a debate among scientists about how worried we should be.

In itself, the breakup and melting of floating ice is not concerning. It makes no more difference to sea level than the melting of ice cubes does to the level of your gin and tonic. The problem is

that ice shelves act as dams to what is behind them, which are giant glaciers trying to reach the sea. Once the shelf collapses there is nothing to stop the rapid descent of all this new ice. This would have a serious impact not just on the Antarctic and Arctic Oceans but everywhere. In 2022, after decades of iceberg carving, East Antarctica's Conger ice shelf collapsed. The Thwaites Glacier and ice shelf, in Western Antarctica is a particular source of concern. A 2024 report from a team of scientists called the International Thwaites Glacier Collaboration predicts that it will 'continue to lose ice at a rapid rate', though they also expect that 'its retreat will not turn into a catastrophic collapse during the 21st century'. If the Thwaites Glacier melts it is estimated that it could add 65 centimetres (about 2 feet) to global sea levels.

Icebergs are beautiful but their splendour is now etched with anxiety. The speeding up of ice-cover loss is already affecting coastal communities across the world. Icebergs and huge ice shelves appear comfortingly distant and solid. But these solid objects are made of H_2O, which in an instant can radically change state and become a gas or a liquid and, on a planet where all the seas and oceans are connected, there is no such thing as distant water.

A23a is not the biggest iceberg ever recorded. In 2000, B-15 calved from the Ross Ice Shelf. It measured 295 by 37 kilometres (183 by 23 miles), with a surface area of 11,000 square kilometres (4,247 square miles), a little bigger than Jamaica. It soon broke up into separate chunks before turbulent seas and a major storm fragmented it further. Proof of how everything in our oceans is connected is that this storm started in the Arctic, in the Gulf of Alaska, at the other end of the world. From there high waves were generated which, in a mere six days, travelled from Alaska to Antarctica.

Icebergs are curious islands: uninhabitable, dangerous and, perhaps, full of possibilities. One recent proposal is that they could be towed from the poles to water-scarce parts of the world. It has been estimated that an iceberg holding 76 billion litres (17 billion gallons) of fresh water could provide water for a million people for five years.

The global authority in monitoring icebergs is the USA's National Ice Center, which, since 1978, has been tracking and documenting Antarctic icebergs that meet its criteria of being 20 square nautical miles (that's about 52 square kilometres) or greater. It's striking how big that is: what most of us would think of as huge icebergs still fly under the radar. Even tiny ones, called growlers, which reach less that 1 metre (3 feet) above the water, about the size of grand piano, are hefty objects that you would not want smashing into your boat. Despite the invaluable work of the National Ice Center, the identification and supervision of icebergs remains rather primitive. As with so many planetary and extraplanetary objects, instead of a properly funded, international organization, the world relies on the largesse of American public bodies and, hence, the American taxpayer. The National Ice Center does more than provide oversight of big bergs: it also names them. It devised the system of letters and numbers that gave us 'A23a'. The initial letter represents a quadrant of Antarctica, so shows place of origin. The quadrants are divided counter-clockwise and work like this:

A = 0–90W (Bellingshausen/Weddell Sea)
B = 90W–180 (Amundsen/Eastern Ross Sea)
C = 180–90E (Western Ross/Wilkes Land Sea)
D = 90E–0 (Amery/Eastern Weddell Sea)

The number represents the place of an iceberg in the sequence since tracking began. Additional letters represent carved-off sections of previously identified icebergs. So now we can understand the name A23a. It was the first iceberg to carve off from the twenty-third iceberg that carved from an ice shelf located in the western quadrant of Antarctica, where we find the Bellingshausen Sea and the Weddell Sea.

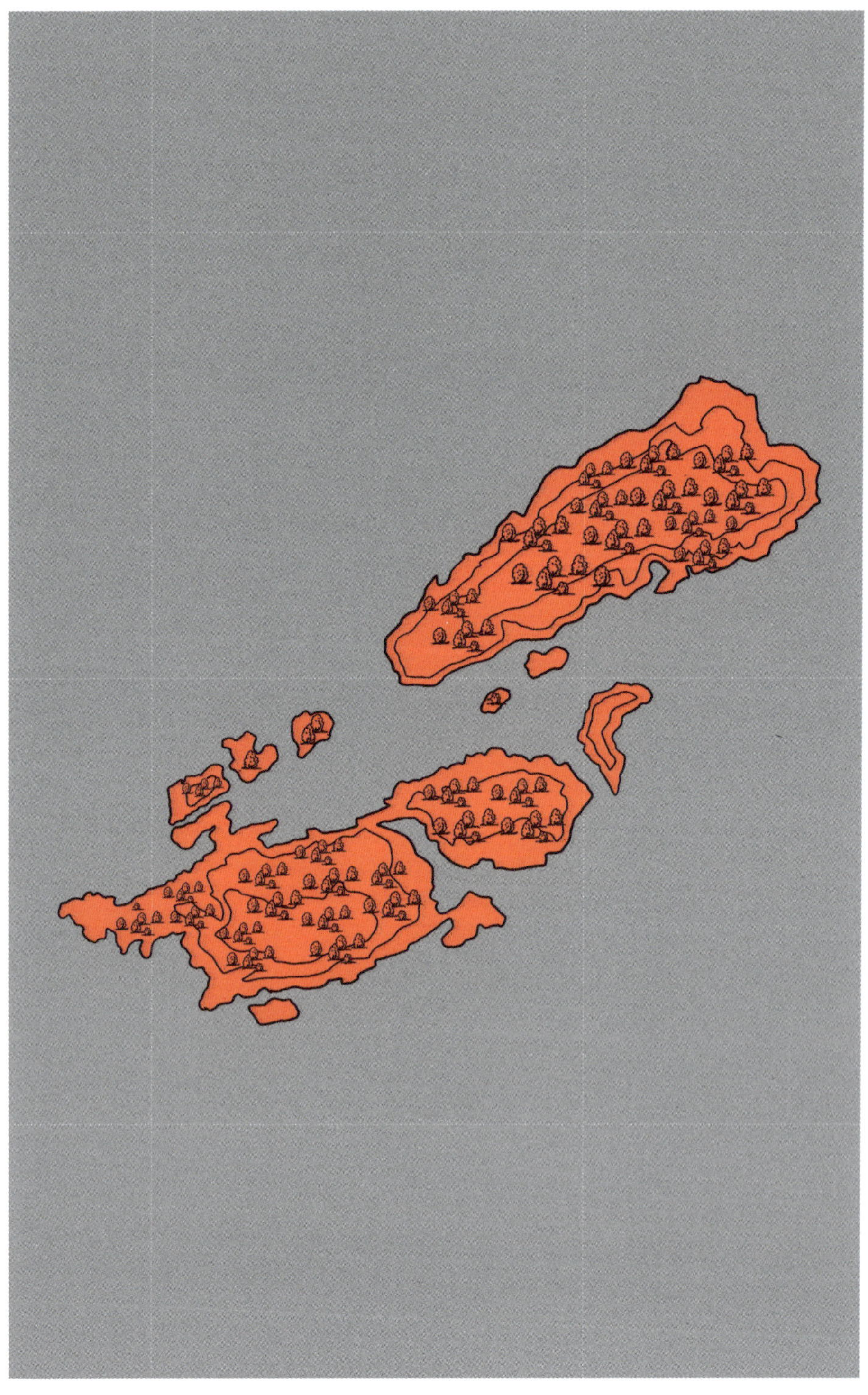

KĪPUKAS

Islands Surrounded by Lava

LOCATION Kīpukas on Pu'u 'Ō'ō, Hawaii **COUNTRY** United States of America **AREA** Variable. **POPULATION** Zero. **CHARACTERISTICS** Kīpukas are islands of safety, created and surrounded by volcanic lava, providing a haven for plants and animals.

IN HAWAII THEY are called kīpukas, a Hawaiian word that means a door or opening. Our map shows two kīpukas on the slopes of the highly active volcano Pu'u 'Ō'ō, which has created many new kīpukas over the past few decades. In Sicily they use the name 'dagala', which is said to be derived from an Arabic expression for 'spared by Allah', sometimes rendered as 'miracle from Allah'. Whether you call them kīpukas or dagalas they do look like miracles: they are green islands surrounded by lava. When a volcano erupts and molten rock spills and coils in profusion it occasionally meets an obstacle that it cannot obliterate. These awkward holdouts become oases from death. After the lava has cooled and turned into a solid black landscape, they remain, providing a haven for life and a place from which plants can begin to recolonize the strange new world that now circles them.

The slopes of Sicily's erratically explosive Mount Etna are a patchwork of dagalas/kīpukas formed over the centuries. Some are now thickly wooded, such as Dagala del Picchio, which has a basic unstaffed refuge hut amid the trees, where hikers who have stumbled over the lava fields can spend the night. Timparossa, one of the prettiest of Etna's dagalas, is another woodland glade, famed for its autumnal splendour, and it too rewards visitors with a quaint bothy. Etna also has examples of lava islands becoming inhabited. The Dagala del Re is now a neighbourhood of the town of Santa Venerina and little remains to show that it was once isolated by streams of liquid rock. In the US a subspecies of kīpuka has been identified, called a steptoe. This is a hill amid a lava field – it is unassailed high ground, named after

Steptoe Butte, a quartzite summit that was once a redoubt but today is an undistinguished-looking summit surrounded by quiet pastures in Washington state.

Hawaii is the landscape that gave the world the word 'kīpuka', in large part because it has so many and of so many sizes and types. The value of Hawaii's kīpukas goes beyond providing safe havens. They are also important study sites that scientists use to examine how plants and small creatures survive in tiny, isolated pockets. Thus, for example, kīpukas along Saddle Road on the Big Island serve as open-air labs for finding out about a range of natural processes, including resistance to invasive plants and the reproductive habits of fruit flies.

Centuries, even millennia, after they were created, kīpukas remain distinct. Writing about an ancient kīpuka called Pu'u Huluhulu (or 'hairy hill') Hawaiian geologist Garry Hayes explains that it still preserves some of the plants and animals that lived there before it was hemmed by lava. Hayes tells us that kīpukas are 'like museums of what once was, but they are far more than that', for by preserving flora and fauna 'they provide the genetic material that will eventually repopulate the areas of devastation'.

Sometimes keeping kīpukas safe from human interference can seem like a lost cause. Pu'u Huluhulu has been quarried, dug and nibbled by grazing cattle, goats and sheep. Yet it remains special. Today its unique ecosystem is protected and has many visitors, all eager to catch a glimpse of some of the island's rarest native birds.

Islands often have species found nowhere else. This is also true of kīpuka islands. One example on Hawaii is a Hibiscus tree variety called Hau kuahiwi (*Hibiscadelphus distans*). The last existing example was found in the 1930s in Kīpuka Puaulu, which is part of the Hawaii Volcanoes National Park, and not far from Pu'u 'Ō'ō. The original plant died many decades ago, but a few seeds had been collected and planted and today a couple of hundred specimens can be found in this kīpuka. Another species found here, as in many other kīpukas, is the Ōhi'a tree (*Metrosideros polymorpha)*, which has gloriously vivid and spiky red flowers. It is rare globally but common across Hawaii and a characteristic and culturally significant survivor on kīpukas. The 'Ōhi'a is a slow-growing tree and a specialist first colonizer of lava flows.

Its wood has many uses in traditional Hawaiian culture, including in making boards for pounding edible roots as well as for weapons, while its leaves can be used to make a medicinal tea.

Kīpukas have been identified in other US parks, such as the El Malpais National Monument and the Craters of the Moon National Monument. Kīpukas can be found in many places and not just on Earth. Anywhere with volcanoes will probably have them. In recent studies of kīpukas on the Moon, a new mechanism for their creation has been hypothesized. The impact of the asteroid that formed the huge, flat basin on the Moon called the Mare Crisium, or Sea of Crisis, probably created enough energy to melt rock, leading to lava flows that buried everything except the hills, which today exists as steptoe-type kīpukas. This theory is not universally accepted: a rival idea is that the kīpukas of Mare Crisium were created by the Moon's own long-dead volcanoes.

The barren outcrops of lunar kīpukas could not be more different from the lush kīpukas of Earth. Many have a unique agricultural character and some seem blessed. The dagala of Bocca d'Orzo, one of Etna's kīpukas/dagalas, is famed for its wine. It was formed when the surrounding area was inundated with molten rock in 1981. That year saw dramatic explosions on Etna and runaway sheets of lava steamrolling down the mountain towards the medieval town of Randazzo, whose medieval centre narrowly escaped destruction. Fortunately, this bout of volcanic activity eased after two days. The main flows passed a few hundred metres east of Randazzo. They did, nevertheless, destroy a lot: farms, gardens and many isolated buildings were all covered and the deadly flows also cut across major roads and railway and power lines. Many of the farmers who lost their fields were unable to sow another crop. But one place got lucky: a dagala was created at the Bocca d'Orzo vineyard and the vines seem to have thrived; it now produces a very pricey and sought-after red wine.

Kīpuka are not just physical islands, they are also states of mind. In Hawaii they have developed from a literal description of a unique landform into a metaphor for how indigenous Hawaiian culture has or could thrive. University of Hawaii professor Davianna Pōmaika'i McGregor tells us that rural Hawaiian communities have served as '"cultural kīpuka" for the regeneration of Hawaiian culture'. She explains that these isolated rural places were where 'traditional Hawaiian spiritual beliefs and practices persisted' and that their isolation protected them, preventing them turning into commercial plantations.

The idea of kīpuka as cultural islands, as places where the indigenous culture of Hawaii survives, seems to have touched a nerve. It is a metaphor that has begun to be pushed beyond descriptions of isolated, rural communities. One of the most striking was called the Urban Kīpuka Project, and sought to encourage tiny 'pocket-forests' in urban environments, little green hot spots of natural diversity in the concrete city. These patches were not exclusive to native species. In the context of the widespread decline of biodiversity, the project organizers believed it was too late for purism. To outsiders, the whole of Hawaii may seem like a kīpuka, a pristine space preserved from the ravages of our era. However, according to the founders of the Urban Kīpuka Project, Hawaii has the unfortunate distinction of being:

> *The extinction capital of the world. Many of our native birds are gone due to habitat loss and introduced diseases and predators. Many of our plants have been bulldozed away by development.*

In this context kīpukas take on a new meaning: the burning lava is the modern, industrialized landscape, and the tiny islands of green in their midst represent cutaways or windows on to what nature, in all its diversity, might look like.

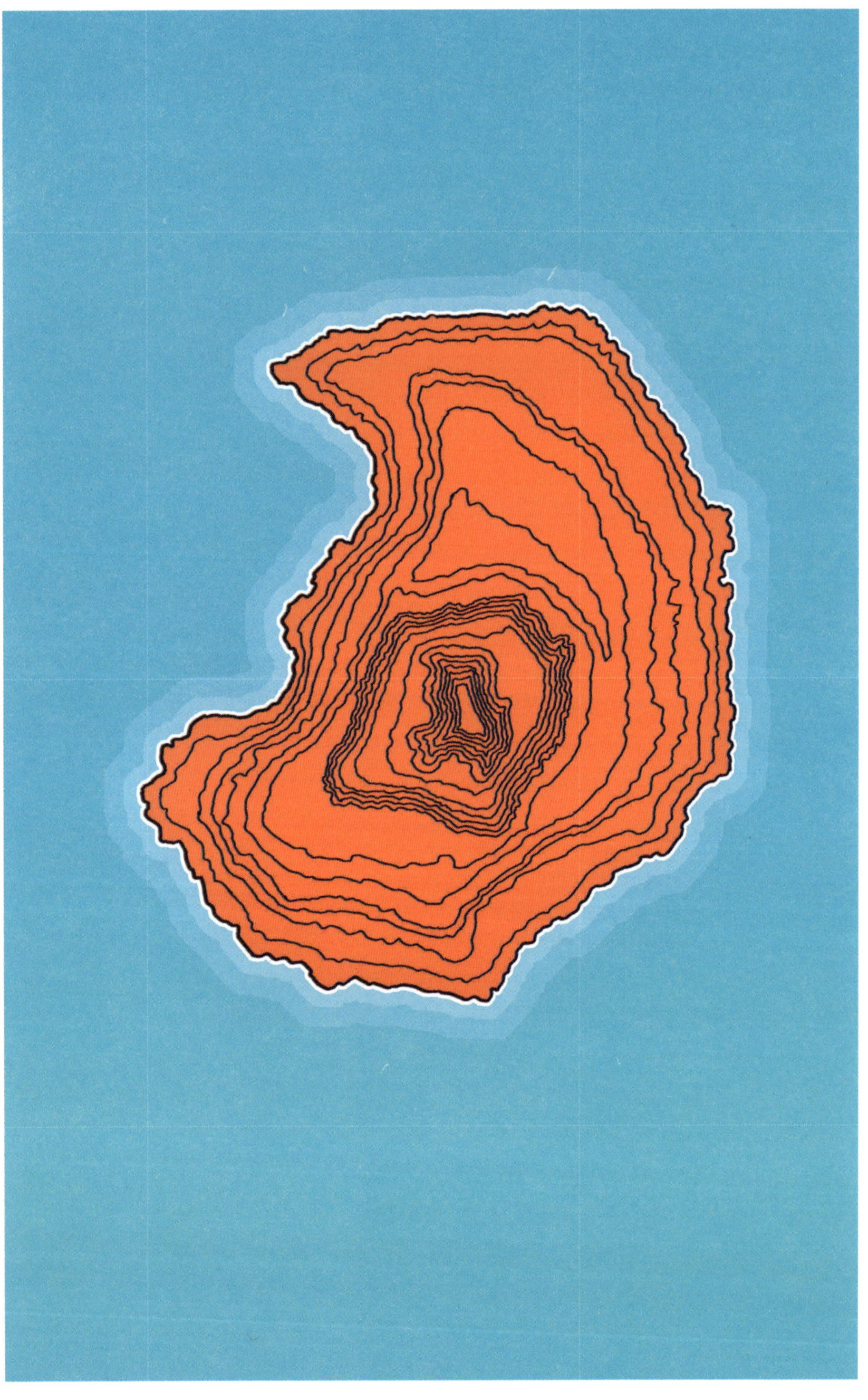

FERDINANDEA

A Fleeting Island

COUNTRY Italy (claimed) **AREA** Unknown (currently underwater). **POPULATION** Zero. **CHARACTERISTICS** Currently submerged off the southern coast of Sicily, but one day will rise again. The last time it emerged it caused consternation and competing national claims.

ALL ISLANDS ARE EPHEMERAL: none lasts forever. Some have a curious character: they appear for a while then disappear and, years later, pop up again, daring colonizers to stick down a flag. Most of these transient islands never get a name and those that do often acquire more than one.

Ferdinandea, also known as Graham Island, or Julia, or Corrao, is a case in point. It is less than 40 kilometres (25 miles) off the south coast of Sicily and a similar distance from the north coast of the Italian island of Pantelleria. A few years after it appeared in 1831, a pamphlet by French Admiral Jurien de la Gravière explained that the island became 'visible from 28 June to 8 July before disappearing before December'. Sinking so quickly meant the island gained yet more names, such as 'L'isola che non c'è' (the island that isn't there) or 'L'isola che se ne andò' (the island that went away).

During the summer of 1831 Sicilian fishermen were alarmed to find dead fish floating to the surface. They had been boiled. The fish could be eaten but smelt of sulphur. These fishermen were the first to spot the new island: dark vents had emerged above the waves, which were spewing steam, ash and lava. The island was described by a British naval officer as 'a small hillock of a dark colour a few feet above the sea'. Over the next few months the island got bigger and was soon 800 metres across and 65 metres high (2,625 by 213 feet). The excitement it caused across Europe was considerable, for no one knew how big it would get. Perhaps a great territory was in the making.

The island was studied in detail, so we have precise descriptions of its evolution. It was circular and hilly; its northeastern side was steep and high and its south and west low and flat. In the centre was a crater with two erupting vents. The eruptions were almost continuous but when they stopped the crater filled with sea water and created two small steamy lakes. The water in the largest of the lakes was reddish yellow and was said to have a spicy and salty taste, while in the other it was yellow and tasted of sulphur.

Britain was the first to land men on the island and the British named it Graham Island, after Sir James Graham, the First Lord of the Admiralty. The French arrived a little later and called it Julia, after the month of their discovery. The Italians called it Ferdinandea. Since it lies between two Italian islands Italy's claim seems the only plausible one but in 1831 there was no such thing as Italy. The area was under the jurisdiction of the Kingdom of the Two Sicilies, ruled by King Ferdinand II.

It was a contested, curious place and its ambivalence added to its fame. Frank Jacobs, a journalist who specializes in unusual geographies, tells us that the island was briefly 'the world's coolest tourist hangout' and that it attracted visitors, including Sir Walter Scott, who 'came to inspect Ferdinandea's black beaches and its two salt lakes, and to dance on the edge of the volcano's sulphur-leaking crater, 200 feet [61 metres] above sea level. There was even talk of building a hotel'.

The Sicilian journalist Filippo D'Arpa, who has written a book about Ferdinandea, records that the island was first officially observed by Captain Trifiletti, who reported it to the naval authorities of the Kingdom of the Two Sicilies, but it was the British who got their flag planted first. The British calculated that since the island had arisen from nothing it could be considered as legally *res nullius* (things belonging to no one): in other words, the first nation to grab it could claim it. At a time before the modern Law of the Sea, which allocates territorial waters, the title of King Ferdinand II to the island was not a foregone conclusion. Moreover, King Ferdinand did not have the love of all his subjects. Some Sicilians hoped to barter the island with the British, perhaps with a view to winning a powerful ally for their campaign to gain independence.

However, like most new volcanic islands, Ferdinandea was made of ash and pumice and quickly began to disappear. By December the island was nothing but a low reef. Sicilian officials 'found only the foam of the waves breaking on a submarine bank'. Today one of the resting places of the island is the Gemmellaro Geological Museum at the University of Palermo. Here you will find a display case with period drawings of the island but also some non-descript black pumice: rocks collected from Ferdinandea and all that is left of this contested, long-lost realm.

The prospect of new land always excites jealousies and suspicions. Although Ferdinandea is self-evidently Italian, the worry that other nations might try and grab it when it reemerges persists. Reacting to reports of new undersea volcanic activity, the British newspaper *The Times*, ran a full-page spread in February 2000 titled 'British Isle rises off Sicily coast'. An Italian newspaper took up the theme: 'A long vanished piece of the British Empire is about to resurface'. The gossip got worse: it was said that two British naval ships had been sent to the area hoping to catch sight of 'Graham Island'. Spurred by all this fake news, Domenico Macaluso, a surgeon and diver who lives in Sciacca, the coastal town nearest to Ferdinandea, got in touch with Ferdinand II's descendant, Prince Carlos of Calabria, to lend his aristocratic support to a 'cultural initiative' to head off the coming invasion. The 'initiative' took the form of a hefty marble plaque, inscribed with the coats of arms of the House of Bourbon, the Italian Navy and the town of Sciacca, and bearing the words: 'This piece of land, once Ferdinandea, was and shall always belong to the Sicilian people'.

Unfortunately, when Macaluso made a return dive he found the plaque in pieces. It looked like it had been smashed deliberately. The cause of its demise remains a mystery, but Macaluso's protests at a possible act of 'vandalism' soon made the press. In the wake of the radical protests that had met the recent G8 gathering in Genoa, it was suggested that underwater anarchists, a 'Black Bloc' of marine insurgents, were responsible. Or could it be the British? Macaluso found the latter suggestion implausible: 'I don't think they could be bothered to get in a sub and go and break a piece of marble. Maybe it was someone with a grudge against the Bourbons'.

Ferdinandea lies in a zone of volcanic uplift and it will rise again, though no one knows when. Chains of submarine volcanic cones can be found off the north and south coasts of Sicily and they have been creating islands for thousands of years. Aristotle tells us how the island of Vulcano, which lies to the north of Sicily, emerged from the sea amid the roar of volcanic explosions. A little beyond Vulcano is Stromboli, which appeared shortly before the time of Pliny. Roman historians wrote of submarine eruptions in the region of Ferdinandea. All these eruptions occur across a large and highly active volcanic zone where the African plate and the Eurasian plate shove against each other, causing earthquakes and melting rock. The resultant magma is finding its way upward, powering volcanoes both under the sea and above it. In the distant future, this process will result in new mountains. The Mediterranean will close up and all its islands merge. These processes will take millions of years: all we are witness to are brief hints and intimations. It is our fleeting lives that frame Ferdinandea as an ephemeral island.

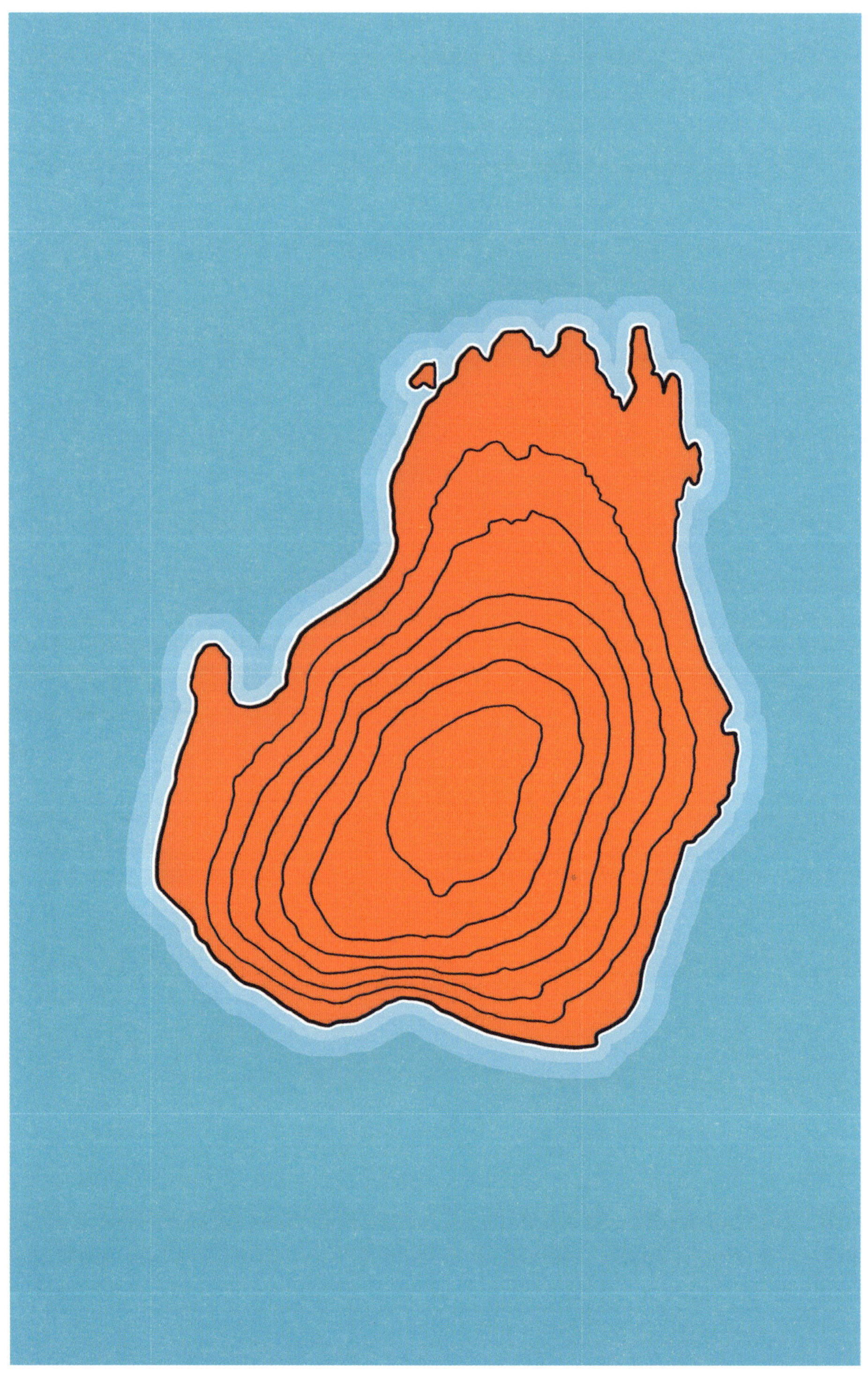

TUPPIAP QEQERTAA

Discovering a New Island

COUNTRY Greenland/Denmark **AREA** Approximately 2km^2 (0.77 square miles). **POPULATION** Zero. **CHARACTERISTICS** A very remote island that has only recently been discovered off the coast of Greenland, revealed by the melting of the ice that once covered the Arctic.

THE FAR NORTH was a frozen kingdom. Across its white horizons little changed for tens of thousands of years. That is no longer true: today it is one of the world's most rapidly changing landscapes and new islands are appearing so fast that few have made it on to Google Earth. Tuppiap Qeqertaa was discovered in 1993 but, aside from a solitary Google Earth pin dropped on blank blue sea, it is still not on our maps. Its story is not unique: numerous new islands have recently been located in the Arctic. The ice is melting, revealing long-hidden land. The Arctic is dissolving and reforming, turning from a no-man's-land of ice into a patchwork of islands.

Tuppiap Qeqertaa is 80 kilometres (50 miles) off the northeast coast of Greenland. It is just 2 kilometres (1.24 miles) long and 1.5 kilometres (0.93 miles) wide and it is a really hard place to get to. It has long been surrounded by year-round sea ice, and dense fog. Greenland's northeast coast is in one of the most remote and harshest regions of Greenland. It's reassuring to know that a Danish team has built a little cairn on Tuppiap Qeqertaa, complete with a Danish flag, into which they tucked emergency provisions and a bottle of spirits.

That bottle may stay unopened. Tuppiap Qeqertaa (also called 'Tobias Island') is not somewhere that lures guests. It has drifts of slushy bone-cold gravel and, if you look carefully, three species of moss.

Much of the island is covered in ice that rises to a height of 35 metres (115 feet). The temperature can get to 10°C (50°F) in high summer but is mostly subzero, dipping into the minus 20s and 30s (below -4 to -22°F) in winter. But for those interested in the dynamic, unruly nature of the far north it's an intriguing place. The gravel and mosses matter. Only a few decades ago ice and snow covered the whole island. Tuppiap Qeqertaa has been 'discovered' because parts of it have emerged. Across the Arctic, islands are being unveiled after spending many millennia buried under ice.

No matter how lifeless and forbidding, islands excite us. Misty, lonesome Tuppiap Qeqertaa, has tantalized adventurers for decades. The island has existed as glimpses and rumours for a long time; a challenge and a gantlet thrown down to Arctic explorers. On 2 May 1907, a Danish team reported that they had caught sight of land in this far quarter, and they had tried to get there but conditions were too hostile. It was a long and dangerous journey – even for seasoned Polar explorers, Tuppiap Qeqertaa can be a journey too far. The sea ice was too deadly, and they turned back. The island is named after a Greenlander who was part of this early expedition, Tobias (in Greenlandic, 'Tuppiap') Gabrielsen.

Tuppiap Qeqertaa's siren song is not a sweet melody but it has proved irresistible. In December 1937, a Russian expedition found themselves adrift on an ice floe and messaged to report a new sighting. A year later aerial reconnaissance tried to find the island but bad visibility meant another failure. The as-yet-unnamed island was beginning to be classed as part of the *Fatamorgana Øer*, or 'mirage islands'.

It was not until the 1990s that the existence of the island was established. On 27 May 1993 a landing was made, though the extent of the ice cover meant it was not clear if this was one big island or an array of islets. A helicopter fly past in 1997 observed that the ice had shrunk to reveal flat, gravelly land. Getting on to the island is still challenging. The ice-free areas are saturated and the ground is a stony quagmire. Helicopters that land need to leave very quickly, otherwise they start sinking. Landing attempts from the sea also continued to be difficult and attempts made in 1998 had to be abandoned because of bad weather. In 2001 a new approach was taken: a light aircraft

equipped with skis was flown on to the island's ice cap. A landing party was able to hoist the Danish and Greenlandic flags and finally determine that the island was a single island rather than a cluster of islets.

Why bother? The island has nothing anyone wants. But, as we have seen in other entries, the value of an island often lies not in what is there but where it is. It doesn't matter that the only 'residents' of Tuppiap Qeqertaa will only ever be clumps of moss and an unopened bottle of booze: its location pushes out Greenland's (and hence Denmark's) frontier. The discovery of Tuppiap Qeqertaa means that Greenland's territorial waters can be extended by 885 square kilometres (342 square miles). That's not much; it is tiny by Arctic standards. But when demarcating territorial waters every morsel can help in advancing further claims.

The Arctic is warming at more than twice the global average. Ice reflects solar radiation, which helps it stay cold. When it begins to melt, and water and land appear, this reflective ability rapidly disappears. A feedback loop kicks in: the less ice there is, the more heat is absorbed and hence the more ice melts. A double process is underway: islands are being revealed and at the same time they are being submerged. Another factor that complicates this picture is what is called 'post-glacial bounce back'. Around 20,000 years ago ice sheets covered much of Northern Europe, Canada and Alaska. The weight of all that ice pushed the earth's crust down by around 500 metres (1,640 feet). Now that most of this ice is gone, the earth is readjusting itself; it is bouncing back. This process is very uneven.

The best place to see 'bounce back' is along the shores of the Gulf of Bothnia, which separates Sweden from Finland. It is rising so fast that new islands are often spotted. Another bounce-back zone is Canada's Hudson Bay, where the tell-tale lines of former beaches reveal the ongoing rise of the land and the shrinking of the bay.

There are many factors at work, but ice melt is the main driver in creating 'new islands' or, to be more accurate, making old islands visible. Various island-counting studies have been done in the Arctic and, from the 1960s to 2017, thirty-five new islands were identified. The new islands ranged in size from 0.4 to more than 59 square kilometres (0.15 to 23 square miles). Of these, twenty-seven were located along the

Greenland coast; four in the Novaya Zemlya area and three in Franz Josef Land, which are both in Russia, and one in Svalbard, an island group north of Norway. Two Polish researchers, Wieslaw Ziaja and Wojciech Haska, have updated this survey and added nine new islands: three in Greenland, two in Severnaya Zemlya and one in Svalbard.

In the old days researchers would have had to risk their lives discovering new islands, their journeys often ending in failure. Today discovery is done by comparing changes in satellite and aerial images. It may be less romantic but is more accurate.

The new discoveries can scramble old geographies. This is what is happening to Svalbard, a Norwegian island group, and one of the world's most northerly inhabited places. The conventional map of Svalbard shows one big island, Spitsbergen, and two large uninhabited neighbours, Nordaustlandet and Edgeøya. With ice retreat it is now clear that Spitsbergen is more archipelago than island. It is expected that Spitsbergen will soon divide into two main parts: with Sørkappland, its southern 'peninsula' becoming a separate island, with an area of roughly 1,300 square kilometres (500 square miles). This new island will be separated by a new strait, running 50 kilometres (31 miles) through the old island of Spitsbergen. This process is already underway and the final cleaving is expected to be completed between 2055 and 2065.

We are seeing the Arctic transformed across a single generation. Many new names will be needed as we re-imagine this vast area as navigable and accessible. Yet these new islands won't be greeted with celebration and fanfare, for we know, and the people who live around the Arctic know more than most, that what is being lost is more valuable than what is being gained.

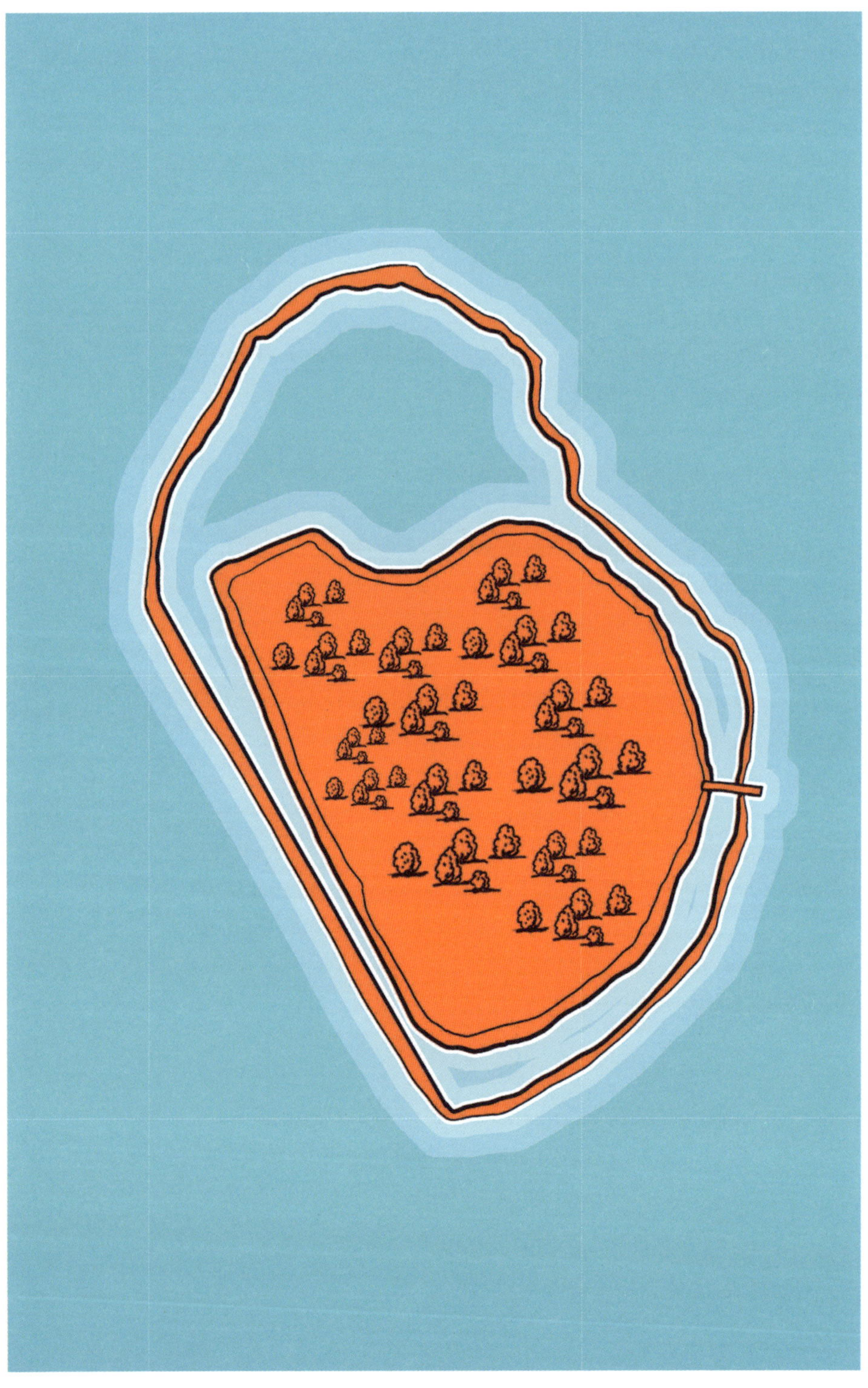

FLOATING ISLAND

Natural Wonder

COUNTRY United Kingdom **AREA** Approximately 4,500m^2 (48,437ft^2). **POPULATION** Zero. **CHARACTERISTICS** A bouncing, buoyant island, covered in trees, on a lake in Northumberland. It has more than curiosity value, for floating plant islands are becoming an essential tool for cleaning up rivers and lakes.

NATURE MAKES FLOATING islands, and they are more common than you might think. In ponds and lakes, grasses, mosses, flowers and even trees can mesh together into a surface that floats and may well be strong enough to take your weight. It's an unnerving experience, as I discovered when testing the springy ground on a floating island in Barelees Pond on the English-Scottish border. Sometimes natural floating islands are low-lying and boggy and, like thin ice, they are dangerous to walk on, but this island was covered in stout trees. It's an overgrown, substantial little wood, which makes it even more disconcerting to glimpse gaping holes beneath your feet where dark roots dangle in dark water.

Floating islands have started to gain the attention of conservationists and city planners because they can be manufactured and, in the form of large floating baskets, they can be used to suck up water pollutants, creating havens of life on dirty rivers. How and why they form in nature suddenly matters. They have many names. One study in Florida labels them tussocks, floatons or sudds; another study, based in the Brazilian Amazon, tells us they are called matupás. Europeans tend to go for more swampy names, such as free-floating mires, bouncing bogs, quaking bogs or schwingmoors.

This diversity of labels tells us that floating islands can be found in a lot of different places. One study on Orange Lake in Florida looked at 116 floating islands, with the simple aim of establishing their vegetal composition; the answer on Orange Lake was, in the main, bulrushes, pennywort, grasses, Bur-Marigold and knotweeds. The Florida study defined a floating island as a 'buoyant mat consisting of plant roots and organic matter' and explained that this 'mat' can be any size, ranging from 'small (less than 0.01 hectare) free-floating islands' to 'extensive, stationary, vegetated mats which may cover hundreds of hectares of water'.

In Europe floating islands also range from just wet crusts to whole woodlands. The only one that I've found with its own name is La Rota ('The Wheel'), which is a perfectly round floating island in Lago di Posta Fibreno in central Italy. It's a pixie-sized woodland, its name recognition being helped by the fact that its lake is also home to a unique fish species, the Fibreno trout. A study of La Rota by Italian ecologists offers a bit of historical context. 'The fascinating sight of an island floating and moving mysteriously on a lake', they explain, 'naturally intrigued people from time immemorial'. Pliny the Elder devoted a chapter of his *Natural History* (c. 77 CE) to 'certain islands which are always floating' and pointed to islands in Lydia (modern western Turkey), which are 'not only driven about by the wind but may be even pushed at pleasure from place to place, by poles'. Pliny claims that during the Mithridatic Wars, which took place in the first century BCE, 'many citizens saved themselves' by punting to safety on these islands.

La Rota would require more than a few punting poles to budge. The Italian study collected core samples from the island that are 4 metres (13 feet) deep: 'the thickest accumulation of peat', they tell us, 'ever found in a free-floating mire'. That is a lot of soil. It sounds incredible that anywhere could float with all that weight, plus trees on top. La Rota is unusually deep for a floating island and may rank as one of the heaviest, but we need to remember that water is very dense compared to organic material. La Rota is probably at the margins of floatability but, as a rule of thumb, dead and inorganic (rocks and stones) material sinks but living organic material floats. The team who

studied La Rota made an interesting calculation about how thick an island needs to be to support 'the weight of at least one person': it isn't that deep: 'a thickness ranging from 40 to maximum 200–250cm [16 inches to 6½ –8 feet]' would do it.

If we can walk on some of them, can we build on them? Of course not. Living on a bouncy floating island would require a bouncy house. It would soon fall apart and probably sink through the island. Like many of the other islands that intrigue us, these are places beyond conquest or colonization.

I wasn't alone when picking my way across Barelees Pond's floating island. The farmer who owned the land was showing me round thanks to a request from his niece Maddy, a PhD student from Newcastle University who knew I had a fascination with peculiar and 'off the map' locations. Our tour didn't last long; in large part because there are so many fallen and falling trees. Yet I was smiling the whole time: there is a childish glee in buoyancy. After crossing the little metal bridge to the island, the urge to jump and poke down is irresistible, especially as the island's trees fool the senses; it is really hard to grasp that the whole thing is afloat. This Northumberland island is designated a Site of Special Scientific Interest and an official report explains that its birch trees rise 'upon a soft carpet of bog mosses'. It also notes that the 'central zone' of the island has Scots pine and that the water beneath the trees 'connects directly with the open water of the pond'. I was just thanking Maddy for a unique day out when, climbing over yet another fallen log I managed to kick open a wasps' nest. For some reason the incensed insects turned on her rather than me. I still wince at the memory. We fled. It felt like the island was telling us something – time to get back to where you belong!

That was a decade or so ago and I had no idea that floating islands could be more than curiosities. They are now starting to play a vital role in cleaning up lakes and waterways and revitalizing cities. It's not a new idea. The island city of Tenochtitlan, the site of modern-day Mexico City, was once a labyrinth of floating gardens. The invading Spaniards couldn't believe their eyes when they first saw it. They called Tenochtitlan 'a very great city built in the water like Venice'. Today the many benefits of floating islands are not just being rediscovered but better understood. The modern use of floating platforms of plants to improve water quality started in China, Japan and Taiwan in the 1990s when floating lily beds were placed on fish ponds; it was found that in water choked with algae and lacking in oxygen, the new islands bring back oxygen into the water and help heal a broken ecosystem.

Beds of floating plants are now being manufactured and installed in diverse locations, including on urban streams and canals, where they purify water, increase biodiversity and delight residents. There are many start-ups working to create them but one of the biggest is a Munich-based company that makes a product called FloraFloat. They call it 'a natural and durable floating ecosystem to create habitat and purify water', adding that it's a 'simple solution to enhance biodiversity and treat water based on the power of nature.'

It's an idea whose time has come: a lot of rivers and lakes are filthy and floating islets could help. New uses of floating islands keep being discovered (see Maldives Floating City, page 52). In the longer term and at a larger scale they may help us keep farming in areas that experience regular floods. When I stumbled around Barelees Pond's floating island in Northumberland I thought it was an overlooked oddity, but it turns out to be a finger post to the future. If our century pans out as it currently looks like it will, floating farms may become a common sight.

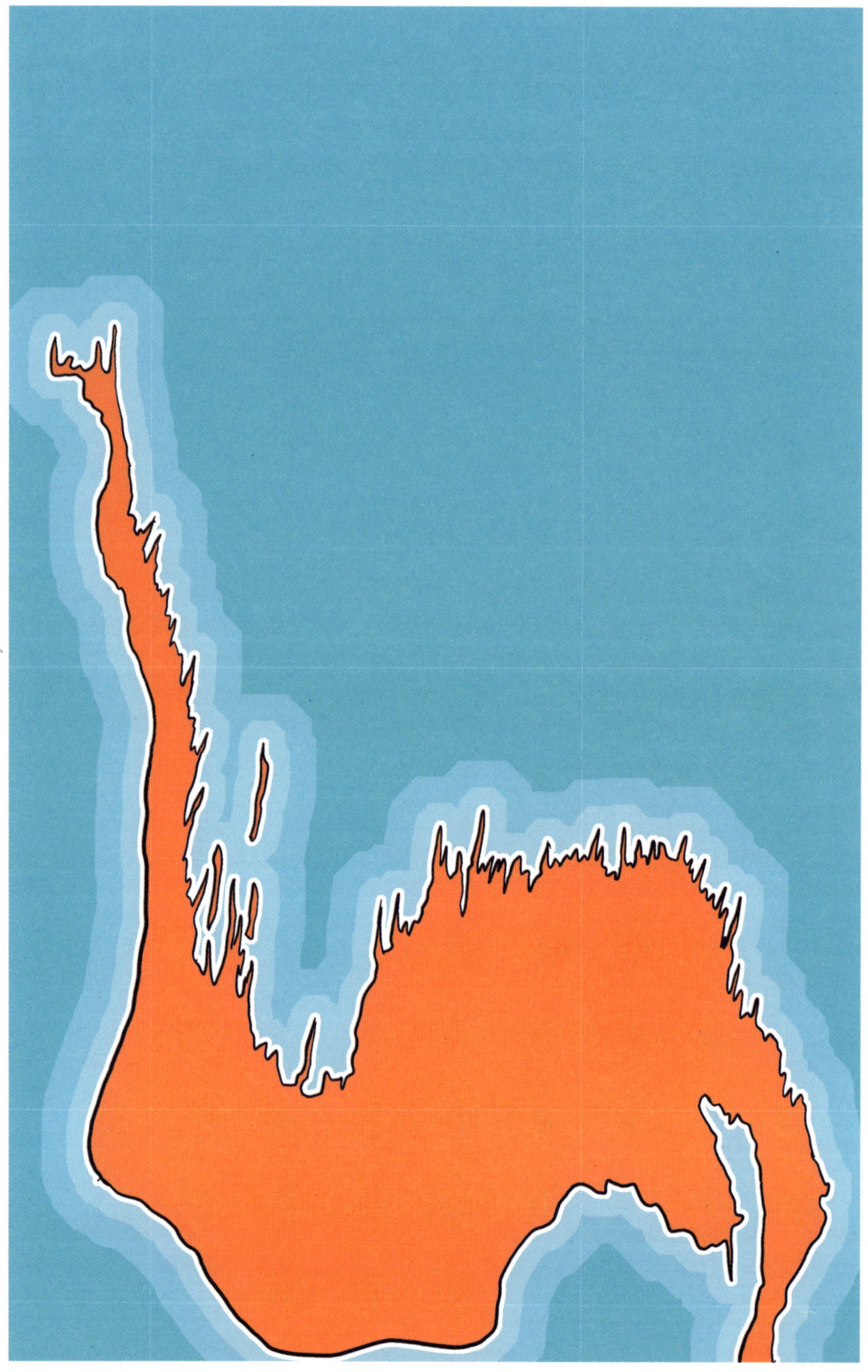

PUMICE RAFTS

The Ocean's Transport Islands

COUNTRY None **AREA** Variable. **POPULATION** Zero. **CHARACTERISTICS** The importance of these intriguing floating islands has only recently been discovered; they are a marine hazard but provide a ride across vast distances for small creatures.

NATURE'S RAFTS ARE curious creatures, pushed about by ocean currents and taking any shape and seemingly any size, from a few centimetres to as big as a country. They are made from pumice, a stone so light it floats. Most volcanoes are not on land but under the sea so that's where we find most volcanic eruptions. When molten rock that has been squeezed and trapped under the ground is suddenly released and cooled it can form huge quantities of this air-pocketed, featherweight rock. The new pumice is fragile and breaks into nugget-sized lumps. These nuggets are not immediately scattered by the sea but mass together, often for months, forming rafts that wander the world, taking a tour of deeps and shallows before finding a resting place on a distant shore, often hundreds, maybe thousands of kilometres from where they were born.

Pumice rafts offer a free ride for little hitchhikers such as molluscs, anemones, sponges, corals and crabs, stowed away above and below and headed for whatever destination the wind and waves favour. This transport system is something we have only recently become aware of, and its implications may be profound. When trying to understand the distribution of animals, how this species of crab or that species of coral got from one side of the Pacific to the other, the answer may be that it sailed there on a raft.

They are not for you or me. There are reports of snakes being seen on them but nothing larger; though admittedly we are only at the beginning of understanding what makes use of these unlikely vessels. The largest rafts seen so far were travelling the South Pacific though they can be found in any body of water with volcanoes. The one that caught my attention was spotted by a satellite in 2021, a few days after the eruption of a Japanese volcano called Fukutoku-Okanoba. This volcano is 5 kilometres (3.1 miles) northeast of South Iwo Jima, which is a tiny and very remote Japanese island nearly 1,300 kilometres (808 miles) south of Tokyo.

Fukutoku-Okanoba is an ephemeral island: it occasionally pokes its head above the water after a major eruption but most of the time it stays hidden. Its earliest recorded eruption was in 1904 and created a short-lived island; islands have come and gone ever since. The 2021 eruption was one of the largest seen in modern Japan – its eruption cloud reached the stratosphere – but was so far away from anywhere that it received little press coverage. It too formed a new island: roughly 1 kilometre (0.62 miles) in diameter. Like its ancestors it soon started to collapse, splitting first into two parts, then disappearing completely.

A large pumice raft formed around the new island and its travels were closely monitored, not because of interest in the life it might transport but because pumice rafts are a marine hazard. The Geological Survey of Japan, which sent several missions to sample and study the raft, warned that if a 'large amount of pumice is washed ashore, it is expected that power plants, steelworks and combustion engines of ships that use shallow seawater as cooling water will be damaged'. After two months they were reporting that the pumice had arrived at the Ryukyu Archipelago and fishing boats and ferries had been suspended. They also explained that there was not one raft but several and 'widespread disruption and damage is expected to be ongoing'.

Pumice that drifts into harbours becomes trapped and builds up. In the harbours of the villages of Hentona and Oku the pumice formed a thick layer, up to 20 centimetres (8 inches) deep, turning the water into a grey sheet. The damage to fish stocks was extensive. Fish mistake small bits of pumice for food, and it kills them by abrading them from the inside. This is a subtropical coast, with a rich variety of coral reefs and mangrove forests as well as commercial fisheries. The pumice swamped everything.

As they clot and cover coasts with grey, it's easy to see why pumice rafts might be seen as harbingers of death rather than bringers

of life. But in the right conditions, a pumice stone can be so covered in living creatures that you can't even see the rock. Dr Elenor Velasquez, who studies pumice rafts at Australia's Griffith University, tells us that when the ones she has researched came ashore, 'they are literally chock-a-block full of animals and plants'. Velasquez and her colleagues go on to explain that the amount of life on a raft is determined by how old and large it is but also in which seas it floats. Large, long-lasting rafts in warm, shallow and coral-rich seas will transport huge amounts of life; small ones in colder, deeper seas will be less bountiful.

Some researchers have become even more excited by pumice. Martin Brasier and his colleagues at the University of Oxford suggest it 'could have had a significant role in the origin of life'. They see pumice as an incubator and disseminator of life. It has the 'highest surface-area-to-volume ratio known for any rock type' they write and has a 'remarkable ability' to adsorb metals, organics and phosphates plus 'it is the only known rock type that floats as rafts' and then beaches its cargo. They conclude that these 'remarkable properties now deserve to be rigorously explored in the laboratory and the early rock record'.

Given that pumice rafts are always in motion and start life as bare rock, it may seem odd that any creature would want to hop aboard. The reason is that marine animals and plants start life as larvae adrift in the open sea and many of them have to attach on to something or die. Pumice offers an inviting environment: it is hard and full of holes, so there is a lot of room for a lot of life.

Pumice islands are not favoured by every creature, and it seems that one particular barnacle, the Goose barnacle, a large, edible variety, is an early adopter and actually makes the raft more stable and hospitable for other creatures. 'They tend to grow all on the same side of the pumice,' Velasquez tells us, 'and once there's enough of them they act like the keel of a boat.' This means that the pumice 'doesn't roll around on the ocean surface as much as it would as if they weren't present'. All these barnacles also make the raft bigger. There can be so many of them that they bulk the raft out into an intriguing hybrid, part living creature and part rock.

It seems that the Japanese raft, arising in the sea near Fukutoku-Okanoba volcano and drifting to the shores of Japan's southern-most inhabited islands, wasn't so friendly to life, although accounts differ. One study informs us that it had few hitchhiking creatures, the reason given being that it didn't cross shallow, coral-rich seas but deep ocean water. However, once it had come ashore other scientists took a new look and found that it was being colonized by creatures from the beach. Apart from molluscs, these researchers found crabs, especially the red rock crab, in large numbers: 'Many crabs were observed on the pumice raft within about 5 metres [16 feet] of the quay, and a few crabs were spotted even farther away.' They also saw a snake that had 'meandered on[to] the surface of the raft about 20–30 metres [66–100 feet] from the quay'.

Pumice rafts have a short lifespan. After a few weeks or sometimes months, pumice becomes waterlogged and begins to sink. The rafts are unnamed bobbing multitudes, some huge but many small, and for fishing communities are an unwanted curse. Yet though we still don't know much about them, it is now clear that pumice rafts are much more than nuisances. They also carry, spread and incubate life.

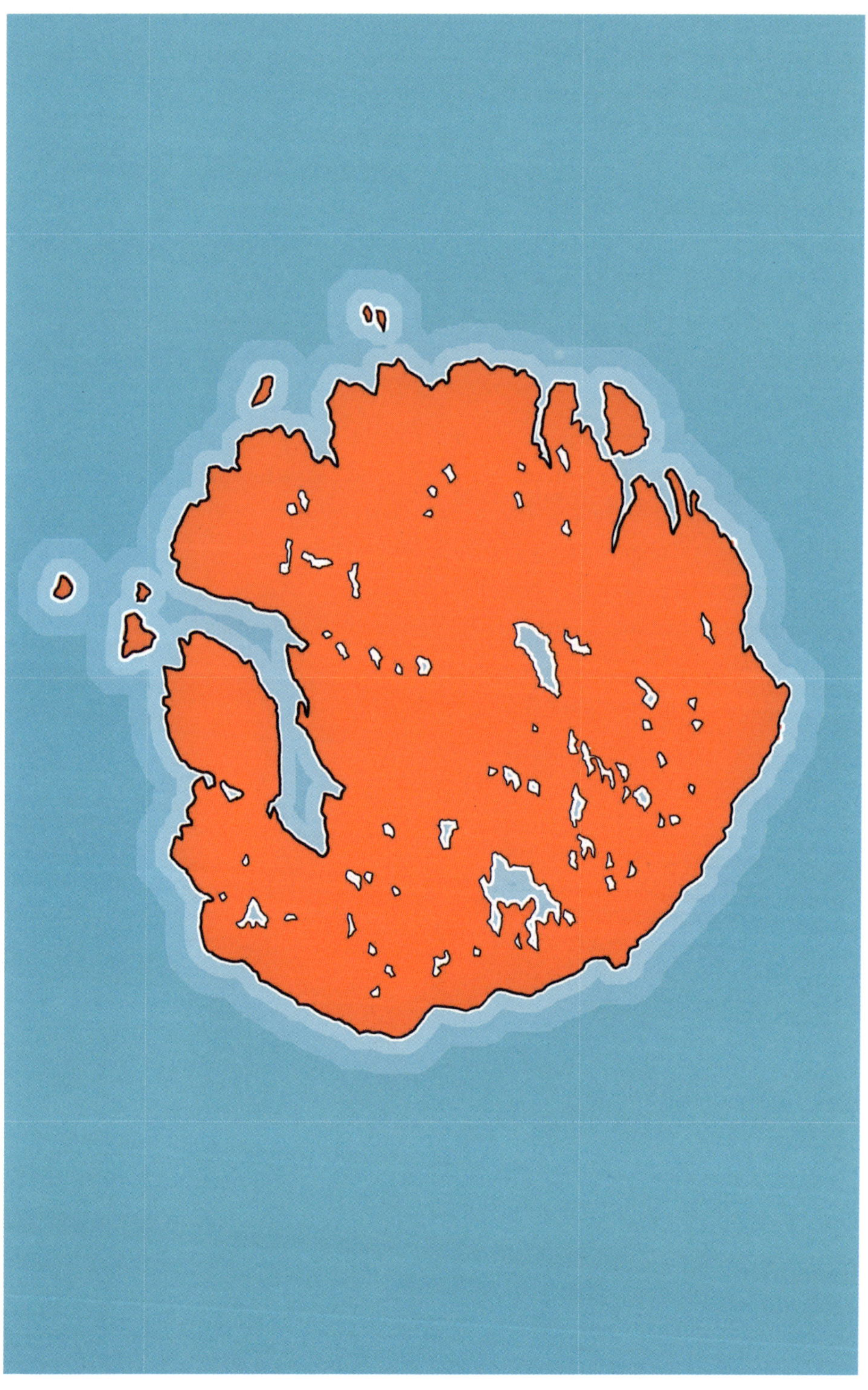

ÎLE RENÉ-LEVASSEUR

The Eye of Quebec

COUNTRY Canada **AREA** 2,020km² (780 square miles). **POPULATION** Zero permanent residents. **CHARACTERISTICS** A circular island in a circular lake; both a human creation and a wilderness under pressure.

THE STRIKINGLY CIRCULAR shape of this remote, wild island in a strikingly circular lake is tell-tale evidence of a falling star. It was here, 214 million years ago, that a 5-kilometre- (3-mile-) wide meteorite smashed into the Earth. The force of the impact turned the rock around and deep below to liquid. It was one of the largest impacts our planet has endured and formed a crater with several rings about 100 kilometres (60 miles) wide. The island of René-Levasseur, nicknamed the Eye of Quebec, is 530 kilometres (329 miles) north of Quebec City and sits in the middle of this crater. Until the damming of the Manicouagan River, it was flanked by two crescent-shaped lakes. Once the dam was completed the lakes were drowned and merged, forming a spherical reservoir that is also the deepest lake in Canada.

René-Levasseur Island is upland, hilly country. Since it was created by a mighty blow this may seem strange. But when you punch down hard on any flexible surface it goes down but then bounces up. What geologists describe as 'post-impact rebound' means that the centre of the crater rose up. The highest peak created is called Mount Babel, which dominates the island. In impact zones of this size, huge quantities of rock are metamorphized: here they melted and were reconstituted as anorthosite, quartz and feldspar. Hopeful miners on the island have been drilling for more valuable stuff: they hope to find nickel, copper, platinum and diamonds. So far, the returns have been meagre, to the relief of those who want to preserve the island's unique character.

The island is both a wilderness and the world's largest artificial island. Despite its size – the island is 50.7 kilometres (31.5 miles) wide – there are no people, no roads other than logging tracks and no bridges to Île René-Levasseur. Local guides can get you across by boat, on to what, since the arrival of the enclosing reservoir, has become one of Quebec's most cut-off and pristine landscapes. It is one of the best places to see moose, and there are beavers, mink, otters, black bears, wolves, lynxes and foxes as well as bald eagles. The island has a dense cover of mature spruce and balsam fir trees, 80 per cent of which are more than 120 years old.

To give a sense of the journey to René-Levasseur, we can turn to the underwater cinematographer Nathalie Lasselin who recently made a film of her explorations of the reservoir. Lasselin begins her account by explaining that out here there is 'nothing but plenty of mosquitos waiting for you' but, after a series of dives, she starts to work out where the drowned lakes are: 'the actual depth in the middle is more than 350 meters [1,148 feet]' she finds, adding, 'the possibilities are endless, and most unreachable'. Lasselin's team drift down to the submerged forest and find themselves in a spectral landscape. 'We reached what we thought is a standing tree,' Lasselin writes. 'There are no more cones, no more needles, but the pine looks pristine with its bark covered by sediments that were undisturbed until our dive.' Her photographs are dreamlike: swimming amid skeletal trees while below lie lost lakes and inky, inaccessible fathoms.

For experienced kayakers a tour around the island takes seven to nine days. The island is a favourite destination for moose hunters. One of the best accounts of what it is like to trek into its depths comes from Drew Monkman, a retired teacher and naturalist who accompanied a party of Quebecois hunters. 'I had rarely experienced such intense silence', he writes, although Monkman admits that the peace is constantly pierced by the 'harsh chatter' of red squirrels and the 'loud whistles' of jays. It rains, it's cold and the island is an obstacle course of fallen and falling trees, but for Monkman it's a place of beauty and bounty. He has a great eye for what lies at ground level: an understory

awash with heathers and blueberries 'so heavily laden with fruit that you could literally pull off a handful with one swipe of the hand'.

Quebec is over six times the size of Britain, and much of it is almost uninhabited. René-Levasseur is a long way from anywhere and no one lives there but it's a contested landscape. The island is at the northern limit of commercial logging. North of here, trees do not grow fast enough to make forestry commercially viable. Tourism is increasing but is seasonal. So forestry remains a lifeline and continues apace despite, or because of, the confusing jigsaw of protections that cover the island. In 1972, UNESCO proposed the creation of an ecological reserve for the entire island but this bold suggestion was kicked into the long grass and a piecemeal approach adopted. The Réserve écologique Louis-Babel was established in 1991, covering 12 per cent of the island. Like the island's mountain, the reserve name checks Father Louis Babel (1829–1912) a missionary who spent sixty years in Quebec's north lands converting First Nations people to Christianity. In 2007 something much grander, the Manicouagan–Uapishka World Biosphere Reserve, was announced: it includes both the island and huge sweeps of land around it. It is one of the largest biosphere reserves in the world, covering 54,800 square kilometres (21,150 square miles), an area a little smaller than the country of Croatia. 'Biosphere reserves' are UNESCO-designated 'learning places for sustainable development'. There are about 727 such reserves sprinkled across the planet, each with an emphasis on research and engagement with local communities (see also Tana Qirqos, page 11). They signal a move away from conservation seen as an imposed solution and towards the acknowledgement of traditional and indigenous knowledge and rights. This laudable ambition also means the purpose and regulation of 'biosphere reserves' are flexible and often unclear.

To add to the mix yet another protected zone has been created, the Réserve de biodiversité de la Météorite, which occupies one more slice of the island. By European standards all these conservation areas are huge and when viewed from above the whole area is just one vast forest. However, the pressure on old-growth woodland, the habitat that nurtures biodiversity, is very real. Louis De Grandpré from the University of Quebec in Montreal, working with First Nations colleagues, explains that although 'logging is more recent in the north, large tracts of old growth forests over 1,000 square kilometres [386 square miles] now occupy barely 20 per cent of the landscape, whereas they represented double of that 30 years ago'. He explains that such 'large tracts are essential for the maintenance of vulnerable species, such as the woodland caribou'.

How can this wilderness island be protected? Ecotourism is being offered as a solution. Uapishka Station is central to this hope: it's a combined tourism and research hub that sits on the main road that skirts the island. The pricey wilderness experiences on offer promise comfort, fine dining but also opportunities to learn about the culture of the Innu of Pessamit. The Innu are the indigenous people of eastern Quebec and Labrador. The Innu's name for their homeland is Nitassinan or 'Our Land' and the local branch, the Innu of Pessamit, number about 3,000.

The damming of the rivers on Innu territory, which produce the hydroelectricity that urban Quebecers rely on, remains a source of grievance for the Innu, as an open letter, written in 2020, to the Premier of Quebec from the Council of the Innu of Pessamit testifies. These developments 'have allowed Quebec to industrialize and the majority of its citizens to access a better quality of life', the Council writes, but this has 'never translated into a better quality of life for the members of the communities involved'.

From space, the island of René-Levasseur is one of Earth's most distinct features: a round oddity without roads or settlement. A deep dark lake encloses a deep dark forest where few venture. But don't be fooled: the Eye of Quebec is both wilderness and artefact. This extraordinary island is both a natural and human wonder.

Bibliography

Tana Qirqos Berry, L. and Smith, R., 1979, 'Churches and Monasteries of Lake Tana', *Africa*; Cheesman, R., 1935; 'Lake Tana and Its Islands', *The Geographical Journal*; Dictionary of African Christian Biography, 'Yared (D)'; Raffaele, P., 2007, 'Keepers of the Lost Ark?', *The Smithsonian*. **Tanna** Álvarez-Nguyen, N., 2024, 'Cargo, Colonies, and Cults', *Kailon*; Lindstrom, M., 1981, 'Cult and Culture', *Pacific Studies*; Lindstrom, L., 2020, *Tanna Times: Islanders in the World*; Wong, T., 2021, 'Prince Philip: The Vanuatu Tribes Mourning the Death of their "God"', BBC. **Santa Cruz del Islote** Leiva Espitia, A. 2012, 'When Christ "Got Into" El Islote', *Revista Colombiana de Antropología*; Leiva Espitia, A., 2023, *'De isla en isla'*; Ortega, J., 2024, 'Protecting the World's Most Densely Populated Island from Mass Tourism', *El País;* Sherriff, L. 2018, 'Jam-packed Colombian Island Preserves Quiet Way of Life', CNN. **Chars of Assam** Chakrabarty, A., 2024, 'Envisioning Resilience in the Chars of Assam', *Routed*; Chowdhury, D., 2017, 'Lands and Communities in Flux', in *Borders and Ecotones in the Indian Ocean*; Das, B. 2022, 'Marginalized Ecologies and Education', *Anthrodendum; The Hindu* Bureau, 2024, 'Will Reclaim "Char" Areas from Encroachers', *The Hindu*; Lahiri-Dutt, K. and Samanta, G., 2013, *Dancing with the River*; Mukherjee, J. et al., 2023, 'Beyond (Un)stable', *Social Anthropology*, 31, 4; **Kihnu** Jegelevicius, L., 2024, 'Welcome to the Estonian Vald of Kinu', *Baltic Times*; Jørgensen, A., 2021, 'Kihnu', BBC; Richard, H., 2019, 'Welcome to Estonia's Isle of Women', *The New York Times;* Cosslett, R., 2020, 'Tragedy of the Isle of Women', *The Guardian*; Rüütel, I. 2002, 'Wedding Songs and Ceremonies of the Kihnu Island', *The World of Music*; Rüütel, I., undated, 'Women in the Culture of Kihnu'; UNESCO, 'Kihnu Cultural Space'. **Samson** Grigson, G., 1968, 'The Isles of Scilly', in *A Cornish Anthology*; Thomas, C., 1985, *Explorations of a Drowned Landscape*. **Ocean Flower** Ctrip.com, 2024, 'Reviews: Ocean Flower Tourist Resort', Ctrip.com; Hainan Danzhou Radio and Television Station, 2024, 'A Real Estate Project in Hainan Ocean Flower Island', guancha.cn; Sohu.com, 2023, 'I Got Up Early and Visited Ocean Flower Island', Sohu.com; WeChat News, 2024, 'A Real Estate Project in Hainan Ocean Flower', *The Paper*. **Maldives Floating City** Adnan, A., 2020, *Floating Cities*, Masters Dissertation, University of British Columbia; Chayka, K., 2024, 'A Dutch Architect's Vision of Cities', *The New Yorker*; Olthuis, K. and Keuning, D., 2010, *Float!*; Treffinger, S. 2024, 'Are Floating Cities the Solution to Rising Seas?', *The New York Times*. **Runit** Bordner, A., *et al.* 2016, 'Measurement of Background Gamma Radiation in the Northern Marshall Islands', *Proceedings of the National Academy of Sciences*; Hale, T., 2023, 'The "Nuclear Coffin" on Runit Island', IFLScience; Hanson, T., 2024, 'Expendable Enewetak', in *Entire of Itself?*; Lamm, J., 2010, 'The Island is Missing!', US Army; Lobofsky, I., 2020, 'Putting the "Nuclear Coffin" in Perspective', *Oceanus*; Wilford, J., 1977, 'A Visit to "Ground Zero" of H-Bombed Isles', *The New York Times*. **Poveglia** Bottazzo, R., 2017, 'Poveglia', CICAP; Busato, D., 2013, 'La vera storia dell'isola', *True Crime*; Busato, D. and Sfameni, P., 2018, *Poveglia*; Davies, B., 2023, 'Deserted "Island of Death"', *Metro; La Nuova Venezia*, 2014, 'Fantasmi sull'isola?', *La Nouva Venezia*; *National Geographic*, undated, 'Poveglia', *National Geographic*; Sanavia, A. 2018, 'L'incredibile storia dell'isola di Poveglia', Alberto Sanavia website; *VeneziaToday*, 2024, 'Venduta Santo Spirito', *VeneziaToday*; Wells, H.G., 1896, *The Island of Dr Moreau*. **Anak Krakatau** Albert, 2024, 'The Collapse of Anak Krakatau', Volcano Café; Giachetti, T. *et al.* 2012, 'Tsunami Hazard Related to a Flank Collapse of Anak Krakatau', *Geological Society*; Prata, A., *et al.* 2020, 'Anak Krakatau Triggers Volcanic Freezer in the Upper Troposphere', *Scientific Reports*; Winchester, S., 2003, *Krakatoa: The Day the World Exploded*. **Fire Island** Ash, L., 2017, 'Britain's "Concentration Camp" in Russia', BBC; Coyle, A., 2022, *Prisons of the World*; Vasilyeva, I. in Aleksievich, S., 2016, *Second-hand Time: The Last of the Soviets*. **BRP Sierra Madre** Hoppe, J., 2022, 'The Measure of the Sierra Madre', *Naval History*; Permanent Mission of the PRC to the United Nations, 2009, 'Letter to the Secretary General of the United Nations'; Ratcliffe, R., 2023, 'Why the Rusting Wreck of a Second World War Ship is So Important to China', *The Guardian*; Wang, Z., 2014, 'The Nine-Dashed Line', *The Diplomat*; Wingfield-Haye, R., 2014, 'China's Island Factory', BBC. **Barque Canada Reef** Asia Maritime Transparency Initiative, 'Vietnam Island Tracker'; BBC, 2024, 'Reclamation in Truong Sa', BBC; Maritime Executive, 2024, 'Vietnam Puts Strategic Airfield on Newly-built Island', Maritime Executive; nhatbaovanhoa.com, 2024, 'Where is Bai Thuyen Chai?', nhatbaovanhoa.com. **Fort Jefferson** Dry Tortugas National Park, undated, 'Fort Jefferson Military History' and 'The Underground Railroad at Fort Jefferson'; Manucy, A., 1943, 'The Gibraltar of the Gulf of Mexico', *The Florida Historical Quarterly*; Reid, T., 2022, *America's Fortress*. **Inaccessible Island** Greig, A., 1847, *Fate of the Blenden Hall*; Lockhart, J., 1930, *Blenden Hall*; Rosenthal, E. 1952, *Shelter from the Spray*; Nosowitz, D. 2018, 'The Questionable Rewards of a Visit to Inaccessible Island', Atlas Obscurer; Rogers, R. 1927, *The Lonely Island*; UNESCO, 'Gough and Inaccessible Islands'. **North Sentinel Island** Awaradi, S., 1990, *The 1990 Master Plan*; Goodheart, A., 2023, *The Last Island*; National Geographic, 2023, 'The Mission'; Portman, M. 1899, *A History of Our Relations With the Andamanese*. **Yesterday and Tomorrow**

Alaskaweb.org, 'Diomede'; Hawksley, H., 2015, 'The Ice Curtain That Divides', BBC; Muir, J., 2017, *John Muir*; Withers, M. 2022, 'Jim Stimpfle and the Melting of the "Ice Curtain"', National Park Service. **Aasta Hansteen** Adomaitis, N. and Fouche, G., 2023, 'Norway Plans to Offer Record Number of Arctic Oil, Gas Exploration Blocks', Reuters; Cavcic, M., 2023, 'Norway Goes on Oil and Gas Spree', *Offshore Energy*; Equinor, 'Aasta Hansteen', Equinor; Fouche, G. and Adomaitis, N., 2024, 'Norway Stops Deep-sea Mining, For Now', Reuters; Kvinnehistorie.no, undated, 'Aasta Hansteen'; MarineLink, 2024, 'OMV Gas Discovery Could Extend Life of Aasta Hansteen Hub', *MarineLink*; Morelli, O., 2024, 'This is Officially the Greenest Country in Europe', *Conde Nast Traveller*; Norwegian Government, undated, 'Continental shelf: Questions and Answers'; Peri, A., 2024, 'Mining the Depths', *The Conversation*; Staalesen, A., 2024, 'Oilmen Step Up Arctic Drilling South of the Ice Edge', *Barents Observer*; Stallard, E., 2024, 'Deep-sea Mining', BBC, Vaangal, K., 2021, 'Legal Status of Offshore (Deep-Water) Oil Rigs', *Lex Portus*. **San Nicolas Island** *Boston Daily Atlas*, 1847, 'A FEMALE CRUSOE', *Boston Daily Atlas*; Chawkins, S., 2012, *'Island of the Blue Dolphins Woman's Cave Believed Found', Los Angeles Times*; Hudson, T., 1981, 'Recently Discovered Accounts Concerning the "Lone Woman"', *Journal of California and Great Basin Anthropology*; National Park Service, undated, 'Island of the Blue Dolphins'; O'Dell, S., 1960, *Island of the Blue Dolphins*. **Socotra** Ardemagni, E., 2023, 'Socotra Archipelago', *The Conversation*; Gambrell, J., 2024, 'An Airstrip is Being Built on a Yemeni Island', AP; Muslim Climate Watch, 2023, 'Yemen's Environmental Jewel in Socotra', Muslim Climate Watch; UNESCO, 'Socotra Archipelago'. **Mayda Insula and the Magic Islands of Titan** Carlisle, C., 2020, 'Winds and Tides Drive Sea Waves on Titan', *Sky and Telescope*; Hayes, A. G., *et al.* 2018. 'Wind, Waves, and Magic Islands at Titan's Largest Sea: Kraken Mare', *49th Annual Lunar and Planetary Science Conference*; Hofgartner, J. D., *et al.*, 2014, 'Transient Features in a Titan Sea', *Nature Geoscience*; Lorenz, R.., *et al.*, 2003, 'The Seas of Titan', *Eos*; Lorenz, R. and Christophe S., 2010, 'The Moon That Would be a Planet', *Scientific American*; Palermo, R., *et al.* 2024, 'Signatures of Wave Erosion in Titan's Coasts', *Science Advances*; Spotts, P., 2014, 'Cassini Reveals Incredible Vanishing 'Magic Islands'', *Christian Science Monitor*; Yu, X., *et al.* 2024, 'The Fate of Simple Organics on Titan's Surface', *Geophysical Research Letters*. **A23a** Amos, J., 2023, 'A23a', BBC; International Thwaites Glacier Collaboration, 2024, 'New Research Offers Hope on Sea-level Rise, Although Risks Remain', ITGC; Joseph, J., 2024, 'World's Largest Iceberg Breaks Free', earth.com; Kolmes, S., 2024, 'Letter from Antarctica', *Environment: Science and Policy for Sustainable Development*; Linch, L., 2023, 'Here's Why You Should Care About Icebergs', *The Conversation*; Paddison, L., 2024, 'Scientists Looked Deep Beneath the Doomsday Glacier', CNN; Sidey, R., 2024, 'Encounter with Iceberg A23a', Richard Sidey; Seroussi, H., *et al.*, 2024, 'Evolution of the Antarctic Ice Sheet', *Earth's Future*; Sullivan, W., 2024, 'The World's Largest Iceberg Is Stuck in a Spinning Ocean Vortex', *The Smithsonian*; U.S. National Ice Center, 'Antarctic Iceberg Naming and Tracking Information'. **Kīpukas** Hayes, G., 2016, 'A Tale of Two Kīpukas', Geotripper; Ka'ahele Hawai'i, undated, 'The Urban Kīpuka Project'; LROC, 2024, 'A Lunar Island Surrounded by Lava'; McGregor, D., 1995, 'Waipi'o Valley', *The Journal of Pacific History*; Musumeci, G., 2023, 'Dagale of Etna', Go-Etna; National Park Service, undated, 'Kīpukas'; Tenuta Delle Terre Nere, undated, 'Dagala of Bocca d'Orzo'. **Ferdinandea** D'Arpa, F., 2001, *L'isola che se ne andò*; Jacobs, F., 2012, 'Ephemeral Islands', *The New York Times*; Franco, A. and Robson, D., 2021, 'The Mediterranean's Short-lived "Atlantis"', BBC; George, R., 2001, 'The Island that Time Remembered', *The Independent*; Graviere, J., 1841, *L'ile Julia*; Camilleri Fans Club, 'L'isola che non c'è'; Owen, R., 2000, 'British Isle Rises Off Sicily Coast', *The Times*; Scalia, S., undated, 'L'isola che non c'era', *Il Vulcanico*; Stopponi, S., 2023, 'Ferdinandea, INGV. **Tuppiap Qeqertaa** Bennike, O., *et al.* 2006, 'Tuppiap Qeqertaa', *Polar Record*; Nilsen, T., 2019, 'Climate Change is Poised to Divide Norway's Largest Arctic Island into Two', *Arctic Today*; Ziaja, W. and Krzysztof O., 2019, 'Origin and Location of New Arctic Islands', *Ambio*; Ziaja, W. and Wojciech H., 2023, 'The Newest Arctic Islands', *Land Degradation & Development*. **Floating Island** de Freitas, C. et al, 2015, 'The Floating Forest', *PloS one*; Masters, B., 2012, 'The Ability of Vegetated Floating Islands to Improve Water Quality', *Water Practice and Technology*; Mallison, C. et al., 2001, 'Physical and Vegetative Characteristics of Floating Islands', *Journal of Aquatic Plant Management*; Pliny, 1855, *Pliny's Natural History*; Natural England, undated, 'Barelees Pond'; Zaccone, C., *et al.* 2017, 'Free-Floating Peatland in Central Italy', *Scientific Reports*. **Pumice Rafts** Akiyama, Y. et al., 2022, 'Observations of Mobile Macro-Epifauna on Pumice Rafts', *Aquatic Animals*; Brasier, M. *et al.*, 2011, 'Pumice as a Remarkable Substrate for the Origin of Life', *Astrobiology*; Bryan, S. *et al*, 2012, 'Rapid, Long-distance Dispersal by Pumice Rafting', *PloS one*; Geological Survey of Japan, 2021, 'Status and Impacts of Pumice Rafts Around Okinawa Island'; Khan, J. and Jones, A., 2020, 'As Pumice Stone Rafts Float Across the Ocean, They Pick Up and Drop Off Life Along the Way', ABC; NASA, 2021, 'Fukutoku-Okanoba Explodes'; Ohno, Y. *et al.*, 2022, 'Coastal Ecological Impacts from Pumice Rafts', *Scientific Reports*; Velasquez, E. *et al.*, 2018, 'Age and Area Predict Patterns of Species Richness in Pumice Rafts', *Ecology and Evolution*. **Île René-Levasseur** The Council of the Innu of Pessamit, 2020, Letter to Mr. François Legault, Premier of Quebec; Government of Québec, 2009, *Réserve de biodiversité de la Météorite*; Grandpré, L. *et al.*, 2023, 'A Hundred Years of Logging Threatens the Innu Link to Their Land', *The Conversation*; Lasselin, N., 2022, 'Dark Time Dives!', Shearwater.com; Monkman, D., 2013, 'A Naturalist on the Hunt', *The Peterborough Examiner*; Salée, D. and Lévesque, C., 2016, 'The Politics of Indigenous Peoples-Settler Relations in Quebec', *American Indian Culture and Research Journal*; UNESCO/RBMU, 'Manicouagan – Uapishka Biosphere Region'.

Index

A23a 148–53
Aasta Hansteen 122–7
Alaska 121, 152
Anak Krakatau 72–7
Andamans 112–14
Antarctica 149, 150, 152–3
Arctic 167–71
Arctic Ocean 152
Ark of the Covenant 11–15
Assam, chars of 28–33

Bangladesh 29–30, 32, 33
Barelees Pond 173–7
Barents Sea 124
Barque Canada Reef 90–5
The Blenden Hall 108
Borneo 74, 76
Brahmaputra River 29, 30

Canada 184–9
cargo cults 17–21
Cassini 144
chars of Assam 28–33
China 46–51, 85–9, 91–5
Columbia 22–7

Denmark 166–71
dragon blood tree 135, 139
Dragonfly spacecraft 147
Dry Tortugas National Park 99–103

Elugelab 61–2
Enewetok archipelago 61–5
Estonia 34–9
Ethiopia 10–15
Etna, Mount 155, 158
Exclusive Economic Zones 88, 94, 123, 126

Ferdinandea 160–5
Fire Island 78–83
Floating City 52–7
Floating Island 172–7
Fort Jefferson 98–103
Frum, John 17–20
Fukutoku-Okanoba 180, 182–3

Ganges Delta 29–33
Graham Island 160–5
Great Andaman 114–15
Greenland 166–71

Hainan 47–51
Hawaii 154–9
Hui Ka Yan 48–50
Hulhumalé 53, 54
Huludao 50
Huygens probe 144

icebergs 148–53
Île René-Levasseur 184–9
Inaccessible Island 104–9
Inaccessible Island rail 105–6, 109
India 28–33, 110–15
Indonesia 72–7
Innu 189
Iñupiat 117, 118–20
Isles of Scilly 40–5
Italy 66–71, 160–5

Jakarta 74, 76
Jan Mayeen 126
Japan 180, 182–3

Kihnu 34–9
Kīpukas 154–9
Krakatau 73, 74

La Rota 174, 176
Lone Woman of San Nicolas 129–33

Magic Islands 142–7
Maldives Floating City 52–7
Marshall Islands 89, 60–5
Mayda Insula 142–7
the Moon 158
Mudyug 83

National Ice Center 152–3
Netherlands 54, 56, 57
North Sentinel Island 110–15
Norway 122–7

Ocean Flower 46–51
Ognenny Ostrov 72–7
Ōhi'a tree 156–8

People's Republic of China 46–51
Philip, Prince 21
Philippines 84–9
Poveglia 66–71
pumice raft 178–83
Pu'u Huluhulu 156
Pu'u 'Ō'ō 155, 156

Runit 60–5
Russia 78–83, 89, 116–21, 127
Ryukyu archipelago 180

Samson 40–5
San Nicolas Island 128–33
Santa Cruz del Islote 22–7
Saturn 143, 144
Saudi Arabia 138, 139
Sierra Madre, BRP 84–9
Socotra 134–9
South China Sea 85–9, 91–5
Southern Ocean 150
Spitsbergen 171
Spratly Islands 90–5
Steptoe 155–6
Svalbard 171

Tana, Lake 11–15
Tana Qirqos 10–15
Tanna 16–21
Tenochtitlan 176
Thilafushi 53
Thwaites Glacier 152
Titan 142–7
The Tomb 61, 64–5
Tomorrow 116–21
Tristan da Cunha 105, 106, 109
Tuppiap Qeqertaa 166–71

United Arab Emirates (UAE) 138–9
United Kingdom 40–5, 104–9, 172–7
United States of America 98–103, 116–21, 128–33, 154–9

Vanuatu 16–21
Vietnam 90–5

Weddell Sea 149, 153

Yemen, Socotra 134–9
Yesterday 116–21